AF498883

THE

OFFICE

OF

CORRECTION

The

OFFiCE

of

CORRECTION

The Calling of a Prophet

Deon K. Williams

(Prophet of **Yah**, Apostle of CHRIST)

kenTell's Truth *Publishing*

ISBN: 979-8-218-74483-0

The Library of Congress has cataloged the Hardback edition as follows:

Publisher's Cataloging-in-Publication Data

Names: Williams, Deon K., author.
Title: The office of correction : the calling of a prophet / Deon K. Williams.
Description: Includes bibliographical references. | Atlanta, GA: (kenTell's Truth Publishing), 2026.
Identifiers: LCCN: 2026906841 | ISBN: 979-8-218-74483-0 (hardcover) | 979-8-218-74485-4 (ebook)
Subjects: LCSH Bible--Commentaries. | Bible. Old Testament--Commentaries. | Bible. New Testament—Commentaries. | BISAC RELIGION / Christian Church / Canon & Ecclesiastical Law | RELIGION / Biblical Commentary / Old Testament / Prophets | RELIGION / Biblical Commentary / New Testament / General
Classification: LCC BS491.3 .W55 2026 | DDC 220.7--dc23

This Book is dedicated to the CHURCH of CHRIST.
(The 'Mashiach; **Emmanuel**: the Lord, (Jesus), *Belonging to HIM.*

*I'm writing this material: because I have experienced what it's
like,* **first-hand**, going through your Church-**Process**: -

(The process of YHWH in which He chooses to help to develop you, by
'sitting' you under another man, who (*themselves*) have been formerly
PROCESSED too. *(St. Luke 22:32)* - *to Simon Peter*.)

- (and) **being mishandled**, *because your Leaders didn't* **know**
how to deal with the detail (of) *you, or who you are, as a
"Prophet". By way, (mostly) of [simply] not knowing WHAT A
PROPHET IS, or what "their" Process would look like, (outside
of what everyone must submit to in the Lord,* Jesus Christ,
regardless of your 'calling' in Ministry.) = "Holiness". *#forAll.*
• *A Lifestyle of surrender!*

(But if the Bible teaches you; that true prophets are rarely
recognizable, or "honored", how does one get what they need
from YAH; while at the very fact, -being- overlooked*(?)*
* [*Matthew 13:53-57*] • [*Mark 6:2–6*] • [*Luke 4:16–27*] *

This is why, being planted *where* **JESUS** tells you, *(not picking
your church, like 'amenities'),* is so Important*!*

You're going to need that tailored detail to get *'through' this*!

You will be overlooked: you'll feel unseen: (you may even 'feel' *to
be undeveloped* in certain areas due, or *just by way-of the lack of
care* you'll receive, **as it pertains** to *"One-on-One" attention [to],*
- Compared to what you see given in 'detail' with your Pastor to
others, (in contrast to you!) Your "calling" may even-be
recognizable, i.e., 'Minister', but the **detail** and **care**, *not so much.*

*While other's living half as Much as 'you', will be your Pastor's
[teacher's pet]. – 'THIS CALLING', is no joke!*
[You will be ostracized: and most people you *go to* (close
quarters) *church* with; – will rarely, **ever** know (Who) you are:]

*As I explained before; You will feel that the lack of attention <u>to</u>,
(make you underdeveloped), but if you go through your* **Process**,
*(you won't be***!***) - Although you-/'ll feel, 'they don't see you'; (or),
"won't Recognize me": (if) you go to the church* **GOD puts** *you
in; (they will!). But may have to appear or behave as if they don't!
According to "Jesus", (in scripture), it's mandated by the* **word of**
GOD: *that if you are a PROPHET;* *[Luke 4:24]; (Mark 6:4)*,
you don't get 'local' honor. And Yet:
You'll somehow, still get what you need:

- Simply being "there", where "GOD" put(s) you!
[That is a weight, all by itself: of "counting up the cost"],
if you can handle this Walk!

-     Prophet, your mouth is LETHAL.
(But *if you Go through* your process.)
Your mouth will become both lethal -and- (**LEGAL**).
(*Without process,* **'you'** *might or* **'your'** *words), carry 'potential';*
(Maybe hit), *Maybe(miss): And* therefore – *makes you, -* "illegal".
<u>Only Legality, "doesn't (come back void)."</u>

-

Hang in there: Don't let anybody trick you out of your spot, ***i.e.,***
MEANING, going through *(and Completing)* **your PROCESS.**
Not even your leaders themselves, (like David's did), **when**
[Saul], his (King), shot javelins at him] -
And yet, not to lift his finger or hand against his leader…
(Declaring him to still be "the LORD's Anointed", *he* ***took*** *it.*
And, if so, - Done with you: {you'll get what ***you*** need!}
Don't **move**!

- STAY *(until)* YHWH ***releases*** you.!

- *I Could write an Entire manuscript on* **Process***.*
(It's ugly, but BEAUTIFUL!)

"Process is a residual that pays you forever."
(That's what the LORD **said** to me *some* years <u>*after*</u> *completing*
my own.) By the time I heard *this***,** I had been pastoring for *several*
years; (and it flowed out of me one-day, as I was ministering to
my church family, explaining to (them), the importance of their
process: - like yours:. (I care about you):
AND you being / becoming AUTHENTIC.

GET READY
I'm about to help Our *Pastors,* and *Ourselves; So, the*
ENTIRE BODY can IDENTIFY, "WHAT" A Prophet (Is!).
Secondly, but <u>First</u>: *I'm writing this* **book** *because* the LORD *told*
me to do it; *And since YAH requires this at my hand, I'm here to*
do What He says, and complete the task through His same grace.
- *I Come by way of* **the LORD.** - *So, let's Go:*
(ISAIAH 42:8, KJV)

THANK You, YHWH. For you have been ([Mighty]– GOOD)**.**

I thank GOD, *for allowing me, to write my second literary piece:*

None of-this would be possible, without **You!**

- FATHER, *THANK YOU.*

Thank you to those who will *purchase*
this material: I sincerely feel it is worth it!
(GOD has graced me) with *revelation:* and a *Lifestyle* of
'cleanness'.
-
- (So, you can eat *off* my plate:) -
THANK you.

...

TABLE OF CONTENTS

PREFACE

There are many [levels] *(dimensions)* in being *a* PROPHET / SEER / *prophetic seer, that* this *book is not the focus!* But the main / focal point of This text:
- *is* WHAT (a) PROPHET (*IS*).

And "It", (knowing this) shapes everything around, *and all* those perimeters - *as it relates* to being a prophet. (Carrying the prophet's mantle!)

So, let's do some groundwork:
-     ***You don't want to miss this!***

(You will find: That knowing *"What A Prophet Is"*, is full of mysteries -in itself- and is in a league of its own.)

Hi: *I am Deon Williams*
(And this is my second book.)

It is such a pleasure to be brought to you, again, in this fashion:

For far too long, this mystery has been left out of the church; – and the "church"; has suffered for it.

—

The first *half* of the **1ˢᵗ chapter**: will be spent on the

setup/(Prerequisites). *Prior* to it, and to that point, **Warning**:

Some format may be *"loose"* -&- (free-forming.)

(As a matter of fact: This book carries so much info; that it became difficult to flow, *(within the regular-confinements of a book format* – you are accustomed to.)

—

In the years (between) 2008 – 2011: When I was with my pastor of 8 years, from (2004 -2012). *Gerald Bess, of New Commandment Church*. A prophet walked up to me after service one-day. After he had (preached and ministered there):. that day. - The entire time he had the mic, he said Nothing to me; - but in the Middle *(of the)* isle: when the benediction was given/-Service was over: **This man of *GOD* told me,** (when I had not an earthly idea: - I would someday become an Author: **that**

I *Am* a Double-Theologian, and I would write the books the theologians read from. (Why am I saying this?) Because at the completion of this books(info), I have no more doubt that the gift – inside of me, would take me to this level:

I am astounded by what *the LORD*, has wrote (through) me:
(WOW.)
Read and see!

Note:

In this material you'll find a lot of what *seems* to be *off* and back *on topic* moments, where I veer from the subject matter slightly to something differently! Those moments are what I like to call *Corrective Detouring(s)*. 'Prerequisites in a sense: Something is being discussed and an opportunity is created to bring to *the Body* **correction** on matters correlated to the Church, that something of the subject matter; *not just the whole theme*, but the topic at the time, brought us into in the moment of the text. Relatable to the whole!

...

DON'T (SKIP)

(The) INTRODUCTION

The INTRODUCTION

To those Who Say, there aren't any more Prophet's.
(Let's do a quick BIBLE STUDY.)

For Most who are in <u>faith</u> that (believe) this, *(as thought out to be an accuracy)*, I can pinpoint *how* and *where* scripturally; *why* they say prophet's do not exist *'anymore.'*.

Simplified,
It's a misinterpretation of scripture; so, let's explain!

* MATTHEW 11:13 *

Matthew 11:13 (KJV),
Says – "*For all the prophets and the law prophesied <u>until</u> John.*"

Though these are the words of Jesus: He did not mean it the way some of you, are interpretating: And this interpretation has messed up the church, theologically, in **two ways**. We'll call them: (Way #1; - Way #2), in just a moment: But we'll come back to this, after we set-up *the focal point, a little bit more.*

"*Until*" - has gotten a lot of people in trouble *contextually,* with *the* scripture not being, *(2 Timothy 2:15)* – "*rightly divided.*"

Erroneous, false **teachings** of the text **is** the problem.
(But we acknowledge that it was done so, unintentionally).
[*As not to shame your pastors, who taught it to you.*]

What JESUS was saying, was that "the book of the law" and "the (book) of the prophets", is where John [Baptist], becomes the signpost of an intersection in history! That something intersected at the time of his coming: where the *NT = New Testament, is introduced,* (in *'dispensation'), and* something occurred for the *OT (Old Testament)* too. *– not* ended perse', (but *"Something".*) (We're almost to "2 ways"), so, keep the above statement in mind.

LET ME EXPLAIN
Many scholars can tell you how the scrolls were broken down-into groups, segments, and sections, and *titled* as such. For example: (you know this), but that the first-five books of the Bible were a collection of 'Moses'-writings, (*from YHWH*) of course, entitled, or called:
"Septuagint", i.**e.**, = "Five Books of **Moses:**"
If you know:
Gen – Deut.:
(Genesis; Exodus; Leviticus: Numbers, Deuteronomy!)
which are called: **"The** Book **of the Law."**

From: ISAIAH to MALACHI*:*

(Isaiah, Jeremiah, Lamentations, Ezekiel, Daniel, Hosea, Joel, Amos, Obadiah, Jonah, Micah, Nahum, Habakkuk, Zephaniah, Haggai, Zachariah, and then Malachi): *those are called or were named, "THE BOOK of the PROPHETS." – And I'm going to prove this to you, in just a second:* [wait for me.]

The *'law';* sat on one end of *(OT),* and *"prophets"* on the other, *('end').* <u>Between</u> them, *from **(Joshua – Esther)**,* sits the **12** scrolls of the (named) ***"Historical (books)"***. After that, The ***"five"*** Poetry books; from Job – Songs of Song.

And that's it: as it relates to the O/T *scripture.*

*(Then comes the APOCRYPHA (original **King James Version**; **(1611)**. We'll come back to that too. – But that's BIBLE, as well.*

(There's been some tampering, just like **DANIEL 7**, says.)

Then *the New Testament* scriptures *begins* here.

-

We'll stop here for now and put our focus back onto the ***Old Testament*** writings, which includes the *book* of the prophets.

[Read Luke 16:16 KJV]
(And "add" v.17 too.)

I'm about to prove to you, in just a moment; That – *(up)* *"Until John;"* meant *"Books"* – not ***"people"***.

(Books of those, foretelling / prophesying / the 'coming' Messiah).

Not the *"office"*, – which ye, had supposed, *had - ended.*

ACTS 7:41, 42 (NKJV)

[41] "And they made a calf in those days, offered sacrifices to the idol, and rejoiced in the works of their own hands."

[42] "Then God turned and gave them up to worship the host of heaven, as it is written in the **book of the Prophet**s:

> 'Did you offer Me slaughtered animals and sacrifices *during* forty years in the wilderness, O house of Israel?'"

(Don't worry: - the *KJV* says it too.)

The Book of the prophets, (meaning ISAIAH – MALACHI), (as one Collection.)

That's why it says "book", *v*erses *scripture* saying, 'books'!

– (That's what it means).

Now *that I have your attention* in *the HOLY GHOST,*
[Let's read] and put some things into perspective.
Grabbing this concept is very important; *that's why I'm spending this time:* I would, therefore, like for us to examine: with a new set of eyes, to contextually dissect this framework!

• <u>St. LUKE 24:44</u>, (45) **KJV**

[44] And he said unto them, These are the words which I spake unto you, while I was yet with you, that all things must be fulfilled, which were <u>written *in* the **law**</u> of Moses, <u>and *in the prophets*,</u> and in the psalms, concerning me.

[45] Then <u>opened</u> he <u>their understanding</u>, that they might **understand the scriptures,**

> — *The Lord's about to get you to "understand"* what you've been reading.

MATTHEW 22:40

⁴⁰ On these two commandments hang all the **law and the prophets**. (Are you getting it now, that he was talking about *the writings of?)*

-

MATTHEW 7:12

¹² Therefore all things whatsoever ye would that men should do to you, do ye even so to them: for this is the **law and the prophets**.

—

' *Writings.* '
(Got it?)

NOW

• **Mark 1:14-15:** (KJV)

¹⁴ *Now after that John was put in prison, Jesus came into Galilee, preaching the gospel of the kingdom of God,*
¹⁵ *And saying, The time is fulfilled, and the kingdom of God is at hand: repent ye, and believe the gospel.*

'C.f.' means (=).
Cross Reference.

C.f., Mark 1:8 & Matthew 3:2 (KJV).
"**At-hand**:" means, '**here**'/ arrival.)

[**Now:** Let's REWIND.]

Chronically; (these things happened first, before the above text, we've examined).

BEHOLD

John 1:29 – 33 (KJV)

²⁹ The next day John seeth Jesus coming unto him, and saith, Behold the Lamb of God, which taketh away the sin of the world.

³⁰ This is he of whom I said, **After** *me cometh a man which is* <u>*preferred before*</u> *me: for he was before me.*

³¹ And I knew him not: but **that he should be made** <u>**manifest**</u> *to Israel, therefore am I come baptizing with water.*

³² And **John bare record***, saying, I saw the Spirit descending from heaven like a dove, and it abode upon him.*

³³ And I knew him not: **but he that sent me** *to baptize with water,* **the same said unto me, Upon whom thou** *shalt see the* **Spirit descending***, and remaining on him, the same is he which baptizeth with the Holy Ghost.*

Let's rewind, some more:

Mark 1:2,3, (7, 8.)

2 *As it is* <u>**written in the prophets**</u>*, Behold, I send my messenger before thy face which shall prepare thy way before thee.*

- (Malachi cp.3), **c.f.** – (for those are the words of *YHWH*.)

3 *The voice of one crying in the wilderness, Prepare ye the way of the Lord, Make his paths straight.*

- (Isaiah cp.40), **c.f.**, - (for Those, are the words of *YHWH*.)

7 *and preached, saying, There cometh one mightier than I after me, the latchet of whose shoes I am not worthy to stoop down and unloose.*

8 *I indeed have baptized you with water: but he shall baptize you with the Holy Ghost.*

So, when JESUS: told you: **LUKE 16:16 KJV:** "The law and the prophets were until John: since that time the kingdom of God is preached, and every man presseth into it."

- The Law were until John because CHRIST Coming, represented the 'transformation' of *(the)* Law, & Establishment *of* **the AGE OF GRACE**!
  - o [*But There's Some stipulations there.*]

Christ was telling you that at John's appearance / Christ's incarnate Flesh, (coming, and accomplishing), - that the "law" for animal-(blood), - {and} "prophecies", written in the Books, of Christ's 'coming', - ended at **John**.) - That *'the voice of one crying' was* in preparation, that (**these**) were *'about'* to end.

(**Matthew 5:**17-19.)
¹⁷ Think not that I am come to destroy the **law, or the prophets**: I am not come to destroy, but to fulfil.
¹⁸ For verily I say unto you, Till heaven and earth pass, one jot or one tittle shall in no wise pass from the law, till all be fulfilled.
¹⁹ Whosoever therefore shall <u>break</u> one of these least commandments, <u>and</u> shall <u>teach</u> <u>men</u> <u>so</u>, he shall be called the least in the kingdom of heaven: but whosoever shall **do and teach** <u>them</u>, the same shall be called great in the kingdom of heaven.
The *ye have heard of old)* 's:
(As it relates from verses 21 – 48). He was *then* telling us that (the writings of the law had an addendum.)

(Hebrews 7:12 – "For the priesthood being **changed**, there is made of necessity a *change* also **of** *the* **law**.")
- ANYTHING that CHRIST address(*es*) directly from the *Old Testament*: That is an addendum, in *action*:
- ANYTHING that CHRIST doesn't address [<u>word</u>, or by *deed*]. - It still *stands*.

- CHRIST'*s* <u>words</u>: abolished, "an eye for an eye".
- CHRIST'*s* [deeds]: (by *the* blood–*(particularly)*
  in this instance), *A*bolished the law of animal sacrifices!
    If **not by** [word / deed], *it does not change*!
- CHRIST, Our example.: • **(John 13:15) 1 Peter 2:21**

If Christ didn't • *directly say / do something that changes*
what was "written *of old*"*; as the* 'ordinances'*, which would*
remain 'forever'*,* (**the FATHER** *spoke),*
    • **they** still ***stand then***.

                                    -    Change: (not end).

(Matthew 19)
16 And, behold, one came and said unto him, Good Master, what
good thing shall I do, that I may have eternal life?
17 And he said unto him, Why callest thou me good? there is none
good but one, that is, God: <u>but if thou wilt enter into life</u>, keep **the**
commandments.

That's **WAY no.1**, Because you thought,
: Christ's coming, abolished "*the* **law**":

-

- ❖ The BOOK of ***the Prophets;*** *(were being fulfilled:*
  because every prophet, in the **OT** *- [*"*the* book*[s] of*"*],*
  - prophesied, He was coming!
    o **John prophesied**: (he / was / here).

That's **WAY no.2**, because for (some),
- you *thought* PROPHET*s had clocked out permanently.*
The Prophet - (<u>*Book(s)*</u>) of, were (*until*) John.

That's *what* ended! –
(Not what you **thought, or** '*they*' **taught** *you*.)

*I just covered "Way 1" and "2"- (Ways), (**Above**),
how the church is messed up, on A doctrinal level!*
" #two-ways: "

-

Luke 4:17,21
[17] And there was delivered unto him the **book** of <u>the</u> <u>prophet</u>
Esaias. And when he had opened the book, he found the place
where it was written,
[21] And he began to say unto them, This day is this scripture
fulfilled in your ears.

C.f. - *Mark 1:15*: (excerpt)
The time is fulfilled, and "the kingdom of God is at hand:"

Basically, because the church believes John's coming was a
- 'done-away'-with,

1) Nobody's preaching the ***commandments***:
2) There are people thinking, there are no more
   prophets!
   - *Prophets weren't done away.*
   - *Just Like the Law ('Commandments'), didn't end!*
     (You mix: the Abolishing ('of Sacrifice'),
     with the Abolishing of the law:

(THEY DON'T GO TOGETHER.) -But- [That's a different book.*]*
Maybe for me to address Later with **YAH's** Grace if He **s**ays so.

The Office of the Prophet... *never* went *out of style*, nor 'away'.
Their assignment in 'that' *(Dispensation), was over with!*

= *He's Here, (**Messiah**) has Come. —* *Signs'*, - *John.*

-

Then, Paul *(Apostle)*, reminded us, that in the N/T **church**, there are <u>prophets</u> for the function of today's time, (also):
(Eph. 4:11),

 – (v.12); 'for the edifying of' "the body"'!

(Which we're about to talk about in just a few moments.)
Pages away, in *the body* of this (work), we'll explore which ways,
 – prophets do edify the Body.

And though Paul didn't *write* the (Book) of Acts:
This is a direct quote from *him:*

***Acts 24:14* (KJV):**
"However, I admit that I worship the God of our ancestors as a
follower of the Way, which they call a sect. I believe everything
that is in accordance with the Law and that is
written in the Prophets,"

So, follow me to **the BOOK** of *the office of correction*:
so, you can hear what I have to say, [from the Lord.]

 = But first,

(The -Apocrypha:

The

APOCRYPHA

The Apocryphal|(*Writing*).
 (Which is a part of the Bible. The same **King James Version** you grew up on.) 'Men', (**like *Daniel 7*** warns about), "added", (in some cases); and like in this-*one example: - took* away from your Bibles; *(to disguise – the* true history- Who the Israelites are. - (but that's a different story), -&- for [Another time].

❖ The BIBLE says: don't add (***Deut. 4:2***); or take away; [***Rev.22:18***, 19]. *And* some people stripped- the *1611 KJV original Bible* -away of multiple texts; that "King James", *n/or* **YHWH-'GOD'** *didn't* underline authorize!
 (So, that means, - that "men" did this.)

❖ Those texts, [*to name some],* are:
1 Esdras; 2 Esdras: (*the same person, who's* 'Ezra.')
The Book of "Tobias"; The Book of "Judith"; The remainder of the Book of Esther; The Book of Wisdom; "Ecclesiasticus"; Baruch (the Prophet) – ["Baruch" *is also the same person who "scribed"* for **Jeremiah**, (*the second half of Jeremiah's* book, life, and ministry). The Story of Susanna; The Song of the Three Children, - *y'all know:* (*Shadrach*): (*Meshach*): and (*Abednego*). *Yes, "them"!).* Of Bel and the Dragon; The Prayer of Manasses; 1 Maccabees; (and) *2* Maccabees.
(It was the meat of the sandwich.)

What Do You Mean?

- (Revelation 22) KJV

[18] For I testify unto every man that heareth the words of the prophecy of this book, **If** any man **shall add** unto these things, **God shall add** unto him the **plagues** that are written in this book:

[19] And if any man shall **take away** from the words of the book of this prophecy, **God shall take away** his part **out** of *the book of life*, and out of the holy city, and from the things which are written in this book.

(Deuteronomy 4) KJV

[2] Ye shall **not add** unto the word which I command you, **neither shall ye diminish** ought from it, that ye may keep the commandments of the LORD your God which I command you.

-

If you take a piece of chicken breast out of the chicken sandwich, the residue is not much to determine, [if person's you are handing it to were not there *[and, to witness,]* when you *took it out]*, What they were they dealing with, in its origin:

– Was it a fish sandwich, (at-first), a burger; or was it "chicken" (in it) (?); - *Times*(*x*) that *by* hundreds of years, and let the "scent" of it/*('s contents)* wear-off; and then we're really in trouble!

Because all I have that was given to me was the two ends of the bread, **old-testament** bread: and new-testament bread: – what was in the center?

- Old Testament
- Apocrypha
- New Testament

[That's the order], • (and) was the Contents:

[Fun • fact:] Nearly **every** Bible-*permitting* nation on Earth has these writings in their regular (Canonical) Bible:

"The Ethiopian Bible, which is perhaps the oldest Christian Bible, includes somewhere between 81 to 84 books, depending on different factors. The Roman Catholic Bible has 73 books, and the Greek Orthodox Bible—without an official number—is somewhat larger, with somewhere between 75 and 79 books. The Syriac Bible also has quite a wide range of different books. And the Protestant Bible (which in some ways American culture prioritizes) has 66 books—39 of an 'Old Testament,' and 27 of a 'New Testament.' –

If one would total all of the books in these different collections, there would be a total of around 100 books, far more than the 27 books of the Christian New Testament and the range of 5 to 39 books in the Hebrew Bible."
Taussig, H. (2021, September 11). *Are There More than 66 Books in the Bible?* Early Christian Texts.

-    (So, I was saying, - *except for the United States.*).
    What were they trying to hide from us? – I **know**. (Page 11.)

Apocryphal writings are the **Meat** in the Bible that connects the whole thing: and is canonical: That's why it's (not only part of the Bible: but IS "the"-BIBLE: - And that's why it's in there: Or, *was, in our case* [to my U.S. / **"American"** readers, (or, it's supposed to be!), Everybody else, - knows – "what's up".
-*Things that make you go hmmm:'*
King James: Stated, *that those of his time attempted to mess up, or mess 'with'; the truth / **the history** / of the scrolls, way-'back* then'. - [It's in the *"PREFACE"* section *of the actual Bible: Original **King James Version (KJV)** – Old English.*

This is the reason (he stated) that he instructed *scholars and noble men - to **"transcribe"** into OLD ENGLISH,* out of Hebrew/Aramaic, and Greek-written, (scrolls) we call scriptures. – *To preserve the TRUTH!*

What you also must know, or to consider is that **KJV** that (We read from today), was transcribed from the original scroll.

So, to say the Apocrypha was not "Canon"; was / is to the say **the scrolls** they were transcribed from, were not also:

Then we throw the whole thing away, *if that* were *the case.*
But we know that <u>the</u> <u>word</u> of YHWH, is true!

-

But (ALL) of **the word of God** Is *TRUTH, And true*!

And the Apocrypha, (KJV 1611), Original Bible: is the word of God: If you say else wise; - "Who hath bewitched you"?
(Galatians 3:1.)
I Encourage you to purchase,
a *King James Holy* **Bible**:
(1611**.)**

If you prefer, "Reads" - like (*NIV*), which, (a lot has been taken *away*,) [but that's another story], - (Just know that many of these "transliterations", (*I say loosely)* - came out in the 1900's; furthest or even *further away* from the *origin* of text: But, Hey.
Do you! - But *nothing* beats a KJV, for our English reading people.

— Thank you:

- Now for the good stuff: *Chapter* ONE.

(Almost)

The
NAME

Though I use the *term* "GOD", quite frequently in my speech; – *(something I'm willing to work on, as my knowledge increases more and more), -* We will capture and honor *the NAME of our GOD* here, *to represent Him more-well, in the text.)*

Throughout *the* ancient scroll, *(And I have grappled with this), - but the more this book is taking shape, the more* shape *THE FATHER is establishing* (that "I" did not see), *related to what subject-matters we would discuss as a whole, while being here*:

But <u>in</u> the <u>ancient</u> **text** (scrolls); the **name** for (what we say, 'GOD', is: (is either, YHWH or YHVH, <u>*spelt*</u>: – Never - *"God."*)

I have come to understand, (using ISAIAH 42:8a, as a rubric, this:

> -   *I am the LORD: that is my name*:

c.f. [Ex. 15:3; Jer. 16:21; Amos 5:8]. -c.f.- [Jer. 33:2].

The original revelation I got from this, *from YAH* was HIS **name** is "The LORD."

But later, (as I began to gain more understanding: *-HIS gift-* to me *of more revelation*), I understood it then: that a doubled-edged sword was at play.

For His name, is, both "I AM", and *the LORD.*

I = *Ha*; | AM = *YAH. - So,* first, *His* name displayed, is HAYAH, (I Am:); and 'the LORD',

IS. 42:8: – <u>"HAYAH, the LORD: that is my name:"</u>

That's what He told Moses, concerning *who* should he tell the people: (*and both* Pharaoh), who *hath sent him.*

-     (*So, a variation: of His* <u>*Name*</u> *will be used, here, in OOC.*)

And most recently, what flowed from my spirit, (from Him, were these words: Ha• Y(*a*)H •W(*e*)H:

Wh = "IS", (revealed to me through the Holy Ghost), by prayer:

Meaning, *(the): "I" – "AM" / ("IS"):*

This is why when we say (He Is), according to scripture, "*Was*" *is never the precursor: (Chronologically, it doesn't say* '*was*', '*is*', '*will*'-*(be).*

YAH is always 'introduced' in present-tense, first - Always!

Revelation 1:8 (KJV)

"<u>I</u> *am Alpha and Omega, the beginning and the ending,* **saith the Lord***, which* <u>**is**</u>*, and which* <u>was</u>*, and* <u>which</u> *is* <u>to</u> <u>come</u>*, the Almighty.*"

(Is. **1**. – Was, **2**. – Will always/*forever* be: **3**.)

Remember, reading *from R to L* in ancient Hebrew: [*humor me for just a minute*: **If** we 'were' to enact this principle. – 'mixed' with *the* modern standard:], "IS" is present then, "*first*" too. | *'A very present help' – (Psalm 46:1).*

(IS).

So, He gave me that I could sometimes call or *address Him* as **HaYahWeh**:. - The 'I', / 'am', / 'IS'.

-HaYaH (I AM) + YHWH- (Am/Is.)

(HaYahweh) • HAYHWH = "I AM IS":

(Thank You Jesus, for your revelation!)

SO, in this body, I've chosen to remove the term, *'GOD'*, for references *of the Most High*: by using what *is* appropriate to Him. - (His Name.)

[*What I would invite you in, (to know about me), is I never jump on others' bandwagons, nor move, to try to seem deep, or to 'keep up' with other people, or what they are saying. - But the LORD woke me up* this morning, *to add* this section, *and begin the process* of *removing:* "GOD", (for *His description*), *to* "Name".] (There's too many: "gods", *and we're going to make the distinction!*
— Dec. 26, 2025): addendum added. - *Dated* for *historical purpose.*

-

Speaking of which: When you baptize, saying "in the name", is only **Saying,** *"in the name":* When *(Christ)* told us to baptize, [**Matt. 28:19,20**] **in** the names of, *[the 3 that bear record]* (1 John 5:7), This *is* what He meant, as an example, - "I baptize you in (*YaHWeH*)" (– **1.**) "*In* Jesus/(*Emmanuel*)", (*or, you can say;* 'in *the name of* the word of YAH'/(God), concerning Him: {Jesus' name is "The Word of YHWH"] • [*Revelation 19:13 / 1 John 5:7*]. (–**2.**) '<u>and</u>' (– **3.**), "in *(the)* Spirit of Truth, (*Comforter*)." [**Name**(s)].

-

"*I baptize you in* the name **<u>YHWH</u>**,
- **<u>Jesus</u>**, *(the Lord, Christ)*, <u>Emmanuel</u>; ('THE WORD of YAH'),
- and in **Spirit of Truth**, *Comforter***:**".

("In Jesus' name.").
In case *your* **doctrine** (<u>*forbids*</u>)
you to hear *Jesus'* instructions, over Paul's.

Matthew 28:19,
'*very clear*'.

—

-

(.)

-

"Jesus" – Why would 'GO*D*':

Divide our language (*Genesis 11);*
Split our land mass*es (Pangea);*

Remove, (for sin) *Israel,*
- out of the land – *[Lev. 18:28],*
(Gen. 15:13,15,16),

SPREAD 'us':
(Deut. 4:26, 27, James 1:1),
all over the earth, to different (regions) *and parts:*
-
Send *our people* to "the States", *(where*
He gave us 'ENGLISH' as our language):

(and–then);

don't hear us when we (call) on the "name",
He gave us, – based on the Region: and language of the
Earth *He* **divided us** *(and sent us)* **to..** (?)

[Make that make sense; (and 'I'ma') keep saying – "Jesus.."

– Somebody,

- *Clap your hands! **

.

-

~•~

Names

•

❖ But remember, (as it pertains to *YHWH),* when you pick up the phone to call your 'mom'; (you don't say: 'Let me speak to "Shirley". Or to your earthly dad, do you say or ask for "Johnny."

❖ According to *Luke 11:2* in scripture, when Jesus (Christ) taught us to "call" on the *'Godhead', by* prayer - *it says, 'Our Father'.*

[It is indicative that *you* (call) *someone* by *how* you know *t*hem!]

It says in [**Ex. 20**], where *(the TEN COMMANDMENTS), are displayed*: **Commandment** #3 **says** – do not use the **LORD**'s **name** in vain. I don't have a coworker relationship with "GOD" (where everyone is addressed by name in the workplace), over WHO *HE Is, (as my* DAD).

• *Although I serve* HIM, so He (IS) - also [my] boss.

Just because you **know** HIS Name: *doesn't mean you should always use it: (don't make HIS name common, because it's* **holy,** and (+), *He's daddy, our FATHER., I'm normally going to call HIM by who He Is, and (What) I know HIM by: (relationally.)*

'OUR FATHER':

[St Luke 11:*2*] *And he said unto them, When ye pray, say, Our Father which art in heaven, Hallowed be thy name. Thy kingdom come. Thy will be done, as in heaven, so in earth.*

(But every 'child' should (know) their parents **Name.**

■ "That's HIS Name, but don't wear it out",

(In other words.)

Balance is key:

[Proverbs 11:1 KJV]

(But remember, you (*Do*) Use *HIS* **NAME**: when baptizing.)

Not His (title), "FATHER", 'Son', or 'Holy Ghost'. ~ "(**NAME**.)"

CHAPTER 1
REPORTING FOR DUTY

** Welcome to The Office of the Prophet. **

CHAPTER **One:** (*1*)
Reporting For Duty

When I was 18 Years–old: The LORD Spoke to me, that:
"I've CALLED you into the office of the **prophet**."
I can't Remember if He said, 'a', *or* 'the', *during the time.*
But:

(We'll talk more about that "conversation" in the latter.)

It is *the premise* of *this* entire *book*:

And I can't wait to break-down and share with you, what
that ***conversation*** was like, (what it entailed), and what it has
taught me.

- [Later.]

 So. - Aside from hearing my Calling to 'preach' at a tender young age, *(at about* **10***.)*
("I'm going to use you to preach My *gospel"),* is what *He* told me.

That's what **the Lord** said to me, when I heard from *HIM for the "first" time,* shortly-after moving out of the Atlanta city limits, to College Park, GA, *living on Godby Rd.* - <u>South</u> <u>Atlanta</u>. (That *faithful day, running around* the bushes, playing with a next-door neighbor, *(Butterball,* whose real name is 'Marcus'). - That's when it happened:

[I knew what was happening, then, in the *moment*: because <u>YHWH's voice comes with *knowing* *in* it</u>: (*so, at age 10:*) I knew that I had just encountered "*GOD.*" – In the form of Jesus Christ, because, He Said: "my gospel."
 - I'm going to use you, to preach MY Gospel:

I didn't understand that *detail* then, until I got older, and never even put it into 'words', and vocalized it *in* this way, until I wrote it <u>here</u>.

It was at the age of 18, for me, that I (then), heard the LORD
(say):

<u>*"I've* called you into **'the office of *the* prophet**.*'"*</u>

I talk briefly about this in:
THIS MUST BE DOCUMENTED.
[briefly, in the *Bio* section:]
-

(INTRODUCTION OF CHAPTER ONE) (Pgs.23 – 37).

<u>WHAT YOU MUST KNOW</u>:
As with *Jeremiah, who was* born a prophet from the womb.
[Jeremiah 1:4,5.], but wasn't TOLD, until he was *come of age*:
[v.4- 7]. So were you, - *some* of us:

Jeremiah (KJV • Holy Bible.) 1:4, 5.
[4] Then the word of the LORD came unto me, saying,
[5] **Before** I formed thee in the belly I knew thee; and **before** thou
camest forth out of the womb I sanctified thee, *and* I ordained thee
a prophet unto the nations.

-

So was I. – [Born with purpose *from* the calling; but wasn't
told by **YAH**, until I was '18' years old.] So were you, my true
prophets. You were a prophet way **"before"** [the] time *you* were
able to bear it.

It was concealed until you could hear it;
until *[it was time]* for you to [know]!

-

That's when you were supposed to (know).
(Not) when you <u>became</u>!

-

SO.
At 10•yrs old - *when the Lord told me He had called
me to "preach"*, (I was already a "prophet", then. –

I was not able to "bear" that burden, during that time,
so, He didn't (burden) me with it!
-    I wasn't spiritually mature enough, (at age 10), to even bear,
     'the information', let alone the *burden.*

I Grew up *thinking*, the prophecy my mother received when she was pregnant with me, was that I was going to be a '*boy*', and I would bec*ome* a 'preacher'.)
—   The LORD **concealed** it.

But after *the Encounter* I had at age *18*.
(*Some 12 -* 15 *years* later, *[somewhere in my 30's]*),
I thought, *(what was a random ask)*, – wasn't so random, after all:
—   [The *LORD, wanted to show me* something].

'Randomly' – I asked my mom, one day: (again; in my *30's*.)
"*Didn't you tell me, when you were carrying me, someone 'said':*"
[<u>Pause</u>:]

—   [later I found out that 'the' *Someone*, was her pastor during the time, and still was, when I was a little boy/*child*: - (I remember this Pastor).
-   *Sis.* (Pastor) *Elsie Stinson.* (**Cornerstone Church**), - Atl., GA.
—   (It was good to see [*in* retrospect], that my family had been planted in the same church that long). They were there when I was conceived: and still members, as I was a little boy.]

"*Didn't you tell me, when you were pregnant with me, 'someone' - prophesied to you, - you were 'carrying a boy', and 'I was going to become a preacher?'*"
(She said: – "*NO.* "). It was A strong '**no**' too.
Then she said –
"That you was– '*a Prophet unto the nations* '–**."**
•   In 30(+) years, - I had never heard my momma say that:

Why is this important: what if I was young and I heard that, and I based my calling, from what my Mama said?

(And although, that's "mama!"); that's not good enough, (to carry you – *through!*).

So 'the LORD', *YHWH*, (though He formed me in my mother's belly as such), **He** concealed the prophecy *from* me until I knew it from HIM- for myself: That way, - no-other *voice* would influence me. And *that* when I heard **the LORD**'s voice and (what) I heard Him **say** - it would be clear, certain, and *incontrovertible,* within my understanding:

- not filtered through what Someone else had <u>said,</u> or had projected on*to* me:

Thank you, Jesus,

that I would know - my identity!

Because *He* gave it to me, not my mama! – Even though she *knew*, she couldn't speak on it until **the LORD** told me, first!

(That's *wisdom*.) *(The mere fact that she kept that from* me for about 32-years; says it really was YAH*'s* doing.

-

So, IF I don't know **anything** else,

I know that I'm one -of- <u>the LORD</u>'<u>s</u> prophets:

And thus, you can trust, what I'm getting ready to teach you!

<u>My</u> • <u>God,</u> <u>YAH.</u> - #handslifted:

On the FLIP

Just a moment ago, (having used *Jeremiah*'s, (and my *example*); I said that you already were born a prophet, before whatever 'moment' in-time, **the Lord** told you. - *Right!?*

Well; so that I won't confuse you, I must confess, that there is another side to the tape / coin, that I must bring to your attention, for proper balancing. This is *[particularly]* important,
   - *if* you are *one of *us. *.*

The Bible says in [*Proverbs 11:1*], that:
'A false balance is abomination to the LORD:
But a just weight is his delight.'

So, before we go further. Here's the ***flip*** to that perspective, pertaining to ***when***,- when He brought you *into 'the know'.*
   – (*For me*, it was at 18,) as *you know*.
   [And even when you "know", doesn't necessarily mean *it's time for you to 'Do'* (in all cases).

   Knowing; [*here's* my favorite word],
   Doesn't negate: - *["PROCESS."]*

Just because you were born as one. Then, the LORD *Most High* came to let you know you were, [*at some point*], doesn't mean it's always time to step into it, <u>*right*</u> (**away**), <u>then</u> and <u>*there*</u>, (like *He immediately sent Jeremiah,* - (once he knew!):

   • that's not a *One-size-fits-all*, type of situation.

   [In most cases, He's only telling you, for preparation to ***begin***, for something you'll *actually*, walk-in, ***years*** later. (*After you get* ....
      "Process*(ed)*".
         -   Personal relationship, *(first)*.
         -   *for* the *office*; or the job-function/- "title", *(second)*.

(Luke 22:31, 32)

31. *And the Lord said, Simon, Simon, behold, Satan hath*
    desired to have you, that he may sift you as wheat:
32. *But I have prayed for thee, that thy faith fail not:*
    And **when** *thou art* **converted**, strengthen *thy brethren.*

    1.   [conversion] = personal • relationship.

    2.   [strengthen], *other's* = the work begin*s for you.*

So. Do you know –

    1.) what you're up against: 2.) what you're asking *for*?

   –   How much do you *know*, about *being a* prophet?

(It looks fancy on the outside, (and *although, special*),
How much of this *responsibility* are you willing to take
on? *(Be careful about who - you're letting ordain (you)*
to something *that* they *don't even know that they are*
ordaining you as! Wait a minute; that's heavy:
[*We'*ll get right back to that shortly!]

Jesus, *says in* Luke 14:28, KJV ['For which of you,
intending to build a tower, sitteth not down *first*, and counteth the
cost, whether he have *sufficient* to finish it?']
(Paraphrasing, - who builds a house, before <u>knowing</u>: (counting up
and calculating the material), [to see] if he can complete the
mission, - [before beginning.]?

   – Know what you're accepting if He *Calls* you.

Proverbs 24:27 says –
"*Prepare thy work without* (outside the camp) *and make it fit for*
thyself in the field; and <u>*afterwards*</u> *build thine house.*"
    • *PROCESS* is very Important*:*
And the Bible says *this* about making *vows.* - *[Ecclesiastes 5:5]*

So, do you at least speculate that you may be a prophet?

Well, This Book: will provide clarities on the subject, *solving some pressing issues.*

To make more - clear:
- What a prophet is.
- *(So, you can gauge it!)*

And so, you will [know.]

Whether you are, [or not].

CLARITY

Most authentic prophets already "know", (even if they **don't** *know,* <u>what</u> *it is): So, we're going to answer that too: with the LORD's help, (giving us Grace.)*

Unfortunately, *false teachings* about what this "office" is, has many, *[plenty]* thinking themselves of something that they are not, because of what was "projected" on them, *[for* one]. And from an erroneous understanding of what *it *IS*.
Through teachers and leaders, who **don't know** *what* a **true prophet,**

(to subscribe such title or function; by (ordination) *to another,*

Is…

(to begin with!)

— (*But* unfortunately, it's happening:)   -

If you've gotten an ordination as a "prophet", you're either gifted with 'prophecy', and they *misdiagnosed*/ordained you: or - you got REALLY Blessed by being in contact with a Leader, who really knows what **it** is, - <u>and</u> they (themselves), somehow didn't ***reject*** you, and "Affirmed' you to your rightful office: ~ #Rare:

Most Prophet's aren't even *recognized*, [John 1:11]; [John 7:5]; [**Mark 6**:4]; that's how I know, ('most' of them)*; those walking around with* (ordinations) & (affirmations), (as) "Prophet", and "Prophetess"-es, are not true prophets, *to [begin with]*:.
- ouch -, that hurts:
Stay with me!
1 Timothy 1:7 *(KJV)*
"Desiring to be teachers of *the law;* understanding neither what they say, nor whereof *they* **affirm**.".

(Your Pastor's didn't know what they were doing, when they Named you PROPHET:) Ouch; that hurts even more: Cancers have to be "cut" out [completely], in order for you to heal:
- RECEIVE this!
(You know who you are: to which / whom, I speak).

[Chapter one is going to be a little longer], because we're only in the **intro**/setting up, Part: The others are getting to the "nitty-gritty". Straight to it.

-

WHAT YOU MUST KNOW (2):
*The first few pages here, will be drafted 'like' an introduction, (somewhat) because *the* **Introduction** has been preserved for something more important*:

Think of it as not Leaving anybody BEHIND.
("More important," in that sense.)

Because we needed to help the individuals: who formally thought: *Prophet's didn't exist anymore:*

So, the LORD, *Most High,* dedicated THE INTRODUCTION to that aspect: and that now they may be able to *'tag along'; and* we **all** can grow together.

To hear the *whole:*

[What the *SPIRIT* of **the LORD**, *has always* **(been)** saying to the church, concerning the *matter.*]

(*So,* **at 18**.)

THE FATHER spoke to me that day, *in a way, about* what would shape my life, **forever**.

(You guys are getting all the juice!)

- *"I've called you, into the **(Office) of the Prophet."**:*
(But before (we dive deep in, let's talk about this word*:)*

OFFICE (Office in the *scripture*)
[I must confess that during the time, I had no awareness of any 'scripture' to relate to, when I first heard THE LORD say to me; '(office)':

In later years, I had a conversation once with a *sister* in the Lord, who was healthily debating to me, *(after I shared with her my* 'experience'), - that she doesn't find the terminology biblically mentioned 'once'. And honestly, I didn't have the (scripture) then, either: (For clarity, she was referring to the word, 'office', and "prophet", interchangeably.)

But I knew what I heard from the LORD in the year, 1998. (long before "**office** of the prophet", became 'a *thing*' you heard on a broad spectrum: and, at this point: I had never heard anyone else say it: but *the LORD* **YHWH**, to me.

- Where I got it from.

I Timothy 3:1,10,13 (KJV)

1.This is a true saying, If a man desire the **office** *of a bishop, he desireth a good work.*

10.And let these also first be proved; then let them use the **office** *of a deacon, being found blameless.*

13.For they that have used ***the*** **office** *of a deacon well purchase to themselves a good degree, and great boldness in the faith which is in Christ Jesus.*

-

Romans 11:13 (KJV).

13.For I speak to you Gentiles, inasmuch as I am the ***apostle*** of the Gentiles, *I magnify mine* **office**:

    (So, we see here, and know what Paul's saying there.)

- THE office of an apostle. (On display: *scripturally*!)

-

Romans 12:4 (KJV).

4. For as we have many members in one body, and all members have not the same **office**:

So, we see here, 'offices'; though some named in the text: ("bishop"; "deacon"; "apostle"). If that weren't good enough to prove to you, the *"office of"* the **prophet**, will Roman 12:4 justify, or, do you no service, *(?)* showing that, *offices* have much more variations than that–that are the **named** particularly by the quotations)/(above listed*?*)

-

And [Permit me to mention though: the one taking this stance: is a lady who refuses to accept the "term" prophet(ess), concerning herself, and must be addressed as "prophet".
It must be, ***prophet***, and not prophetess.

And - where is that -in the Bible, - (But I'm actually bringing this up or highlighting it to share a point of hers, - not discredit: (one moment!)

Having my own experience around 1998, hearing this from the LORD, Himself: [Now], in recent years, I've heard many others, now use this terminology, "**office**".

I find it interesting, that people of a different background, geographical location, and who I haven't shared coffee, or as much as the same room with, <u>in recent years</u>, are Now saying the same thing), - 'office', (of the prophet), *long after* my experience.

I don't have to copycat! - Them saying it, is not what makes it authentic: WHO Said it to me, (does!) – *The LORD.*
[In the year of 1998].

(I will say this), it was revealed to me in recent years. On the title page, I've stated something: something that was revealed to me, pertaining to myself: that I am a "prophet of the Most High / and an apostle of Christ": -

I have discovered that there are some 'old-school', prophet/seers, amidst, (still) from the womb. Such as I and others. Who like– (Prophets who walked the earth prior to the revealing of Christ-in-flesh, prior to the outpouring of the Spirit *Himself by* the in-dwelling of the Holy Ghost, with fire… (*I'm in no way saying we're anything without the HOLY GHOST: (And I'd be dead without him:*)

The Bible recognizes; there is a "power" of the prophet. A New Testament (N.T.) text, with an old-school / Old Testament (O.T.) implication: *times prior to the Spirit's indwelling revealing.*

There was a "a spirit, and a power, of a prophet", specifically referencing "Elijah", during this text found in St. Luke 1:17 (KJV).

And (then), there are, "prophet's" *through* (or *of*) the "five fold" ministering gifts, - I will, (pertaining to the woman of *Yah,* mentioned earlier), [say this],.. She may have a point!

If she received her prophet-hood through the five-fold, then that means she may declare a non-genderism role, to the function: (Prophet). Maybe she has a point there:

[and *the Lord* told me not to minimize what her experience was:]. I'm inclined to believe that a female + prophet (=) 'prophetess'. Like the Bible shows.

(But I heard the voice of YAH too.) When He told me not to call into question, her "experience."

-

Back To The Beginning
So. - "office of the prophet."
My next moment was a wisdom that couldn't attribute to my own, (and especially at such a young age), to not know the powerful implication of my next response:

I **said** to Him! It was in *question* and both, *statement* format: (*which you'll get the rest, later.*) - I said this to the Lord:

(?!) -, "What does a prophet do(?).

I had no clue what a prophet was. *Never, (that I know* of), had I even heard the terminology, "prophet", during that time, (even though I grew up heavily, in the church.

The LORD{'s} immediate response, and the results of this moment, would set me up for a lifetime. To follow this path Correctly.

And that answer set me up for a lifetime of blessing, to begin my journey, properly, into the *lifestyle* and the **official** <u>training</u> of being (O)ne *of* HIS prophets.

-

(I'm Going to say this as a *prerequisite* to something else!)

Though, I grew up in church, - the Lord told me, during the age *of* about 20 /21,

 "You are now of age, where I don't require you to follow your family" (anymore): - *I'm going to give you your own pastor:"*.

WHATS THE RUBRIC -?

Let me encourage you, my training was of **the LORD**, and a 'God'-thing, because He kept me away from prophetic and *(openly)* apostolic houses, through my entire journey of being in church, under the leadership of "another".

= "<u>My Pastor/s</u>", (prior to m*e* pastoring).

Why is this encouraging, because most people believe that the true evidence that they heard the Lord say or nudge them into the *'office of the prophet'*, is for *YHWH* to set them/[*you*] in [*to*], "a prophetic house", *to train you*, right?! Afterall, it's biblically-correct, (somewhat!)? – those were not pastors.

In (I Samuel 10:5, 10) - The prophets of-old attended the school, or *'company'* of the prophets, - (not the **church** of the prophets)! They *learned*, in *tutelage*, how to be… (think;.. "the *company* of the prophets, also who followed Elisha around: (Referencing II Kings 2:3,5,7, - With "Elijah", as head:

(We talk More in depth about these schools *later, too.)*

-

To my own frustration, I wanted to be taught by my *"pastor(s)"*, and even be 'unlocked' to what I was called to, but my entirety of being in church in my 'adult' years, **from age 20** – (36), when I started pastoring, ***at that*** (age), - (not counting the time "I grew up in the church", but from the time when I was given *my* (own) first pastor, (At twenty years old that *The LORD* had for 'me'.)

(I was never given a prophet / as one of my pastor's, to train me.)

But sitting in a prophetic house is **not** your evidence. 'YHWH Said', *is your evidence*. As a matter of fact, sitting in a 'prophetic house' can be very dangerous, [if you're not careful]. What I mean by this, and (*how* I know this), is by way of another conversation with the *Master*.

Years later, I fervently, *from my heart* inquired of the LORD, 'why would you call me to the *office of the prophet,* but then never set me in a <u>prophetic</u> <u>house</u>?'- (speaking in reference to church attendance and whose your pastor), He explained to me, - because He gave me the greater portion; character, the importance of relationship, etc., (all these things I got from my **3** Pastors over my journey, "Foster", "Bess", (finally. "Durrah,")).
He *explained it to me*, [like this]; that if He had Sat me in a 'prophetic house' I would'*ve* wound up a hypocrite, like many others.

<u>**Now**</u>, this by far is not a statement against the prophetic houses, pastors, or processes, - but what He **explained** to me, is that <u>there,</u> (*in many cases)* is such an emphasis on learning how to "prophesy"; here it is again, - that *if you're not careful*, you can become skillful, but not in character to stand in the consecration *of* your office. In integrity - (much greater than the Gift.) Especially when people are ill-prepared to even know "what is a prophet for", in the first place.

'*(All the prerequisites are over).* '

Go with me…

HELLO

I'm writing this "letter", because the Body of Christ is
deficient in a spiritual nutrition that only comes from or through:
THE PROPHET:

-

(The Office of the Prophet.)

-

Gift's. *I need you to sit this one out*!
(But I ask you to join in - as a participating *Listener*.)
You are valuable: and *needed:* but your 'function' in *operation,*
has been misrepresented as "**our**s", for far *too* long:
So, sit this one out. (But do listen), please. (I ask you).
- *To Those: who (walk-in) and carry / the gift of prophecy.*

"I've called you, into the 'office of the Prophet.'"
That's what the Lord, said to me:
- *and we'll **cover** that, (and) go Beyond:*

-

Dictionary.com definition.

Office:

*"a position of duty, trust, or <u>authority</u>, especially <u>in</u> the
<u>government</u>, a corporation, a society, or the like:"*

OFFICERS

Did you know that the kingdom of Heaven is a government *in/of itself? I mean; it is the* Government of all governments!

> *ISAIAH 9:6* <u>*King James Bible*</u> *(KJV)*
> *"For unto us a child is born, unto us a son is given: and the government shall be upon his shoulder: and his name shall be called Wonderful, Counseller, The mighty God, The everlasting Father, The Prince of Peace."*

Kingdom*:* <u>*dictionary.com*</u>
> *1) A state or **government** having a king or a queen as its head.*
> *5) The spiritual sovereignty of God (**YAH**) or Christ.*
> *6) The domain over which the spiritual sovereignty of God or Christ* (Yahushua) *extends, whether in heaven or on earth.*

So, in essence, a prophet (of the Most High), serves the 'duty' somewhat of a spiritual Police OFFICE(r).. To enforce the heart, mind, and intent of YHWH. It serves in the stead of the biblical Judge, but now differently (historically speaking), from the time of the administration of "Judges":
(See Book of Judges *and* Exodus 18.*)*

Prophets are not the judges - but are announcers of the 'judgement' /(decision) come from *(YHWH)*, our 'Judge.'

Because *YHVH* is gracious, *those same mouthpieces, give warning of what can be corrected or rectified, in order to prevent the **verdict** that has been decided (it **would** be) if no changes were or are made.*

(We will revisit this soon, most certainly!)

The lack of understanding of what a true prophet is, and thus, the lack of (its) *active presence; (meaning ʿoperation ʾ). And in its proper place, -flowing-, is the reason the* Body of Christ *is in the poor shape that (she) is in!*

Sin has run amuck. Even Jesus subjected himself to the natural laws put in place, when He rendered unto Caesar what was Caesar's... therefore, the **stop light** *has its place on our roads, right?-It prevents calamity and creates order on our streets and at our intersections. And when we fail to keep the order, there are 'government' officials there, to ticket, WARN, punish, and or Remind us ...*
(Sometimes even through those punishments),
- that we have broke'n *The LAW!*

-

*When we; (**pastors** even), don't understand (who) and what a prophet's job is, (and if not understanding), thus, mistaking something else for that function,*

then what else are we to expect in the Body of Christ, but a bunch of 'accidents', taking place(?)

A whole bunch of sin, a whole bunch of flesh, a whole bunch of 'form/s' of godliness', hypocrisy, and a whole big bunches' of 'mess'.
-
(When order is not set, in the house/church, as a whole!)

Before we proceed; **two** *(1 -2) things!*
Let me work my way backwards.

-;-

1: The pastor's particularly (not all, *but most*), and leaders, as I mentioned above, 'not understanding'.

(Too long, are there spiritual leaders running churches, pastoring us, and "watching for our souls", who can't handle raising up prophets in their midst, because they don't even know what one is themselves.)

The Gift of Prophecy does not make One a prophet. There are "gifts of prophecy's (right) (now), who are out there, ordained, installed, affirmed: or (whatever type of term), we *would like to use: -as-* "Prophet" *So- and -So*, and Prophetess - *Such*. MEANWHILE (someone would say, 'back at the ranch'.)

But in Reality, somewhere, in the 'BACK of the Church', are the true prophet's and prophetesses**'** of the **Most High** the Creator, (whose Pastors' have not a clue who they, or (you) are… (in some cases],

(*And in some case, they do, and still will not *recognize* "you".)*

(I can speak this way and it not be demeaning of our Pastors, seeing that, as being one, *myself, I can't legitimately be talking "down" on Something I am.). And rejoice in being!*

(I'm addressing what we lack. Not the role, 'Pastor' itself.)
I think this gives me a little bit more room for grace to speak this way, and a greenlight from an observation, **first:** *(before Pastoring; but already being a prophet),* **-and-** *by being a pastor (now), for nearly a decade at this point: while remaining (a) Prophet of* **YAH**.

I'm not coming against (pastoral/ship), myself, or others who occupy the role, as pastor, but I'm a **prophet** first: and something needs, "corrected." - I have something credible to say about this aspect: being, both pastor & prophet. *(And a disciple* of Christ, (no titles needed), who went through my full process in *the church,* *(before I became a Pastor.)*

-

*You're invisible, while other people who YAH didn't sanction to walk in that power, Carries, (**watch this**), - YOUR "badge", [officer].*

> *They have your "title". – But* You *have the authority.*

(Full* scope. *[And* for **clarity]: I fully believe in ordination: It is needed to allow Earth to agree with what Heaven has said. That's not the problem! (I'm BIG on **Process**): The problem is in Making Sure we are ordaining appropriately. And **we** are failing at that: (really important). •**Remember** 1 Tim.1:7*

....

Real prophets don't prophesy to individuals much. When we are hearing the prophetic, it is usually for a whole church, nation, or group of people. (***We'll come back to this too****:)*

And usually when we prophet's do have a word [of prophecy] for *an individual,* that individual is a man of authority that has other people under him, such as kings, priests, leaders, and Pastor's! Thus, the LORD sends the prophet in to the **Head** of those people. (*For, if* order starts at the Head, it will spill down upon/*to* the people: [from the leader] that *YHWH* spoke 'to' personally, through the mouthpiece of the prophet, (*His* servants.)

If you can tell an individual Yhwh is going to give them a house, there's a 94.8471(%)-percent chance, that you carry the Gift [of the Spirit], of 'prophecy'. You are not, a PRO P HET.

(That doesn't in any way, make you an "Officer of the Law" of the LORD. – The [Lord's Word or command]!)

2: When I said that Jesus the Messiah; (the same Person as Yahushua ha Mashiach), obeyed the *laws of the land:* let's put that *in greater context, please!*

[THIS IS GOOD. Watch this.]
*We obey the laws of the land (Earth), AS LONG AS they don't conflict with the laws of the kingdom of **Heaven**.*

Need an example?

Daniel, Hananiah, Mishael, and Azariah, (on multiple or separate accounts) *were faced with 'a law' that was passed in the land of Babylon, etc., by the ruling officials; the law passers, themselves,* [in one example] *Nebuchadnezzar... And [others like Darius], but because the law passed, was blasphemous, and* **it** *directly opposed the law of the LORD, (Commandments #1, and #2), [Ex. 20:]. There was and will forever be a reason, legitimately, to break '**the law***'[s] of the land. To keep them of* the *FATHER when they dare stan*ce, *or* go up *against our God.*

Commandment No. *1. (Exodus 20:3)*

"Thou shalt have no other gods before ME."

Commandment No. *2. (Exodus 20:4-6)*

4. *Thou shalt not make unto you any graven image, or any likeness of anything that is in heaven above, or that is in the earth beneath, or that is in the waters under the earth:* **5. Thou shalt not bow down thyself to them,** *nor serve them: for I the LORD thy God am* *a jealous God, (visiting the iniquity of the fathers upon the children unto the third and fourth generation of them that hate me;)* **6.** *And shewing mercy unto thousands of them that love me,* **and keep my commandments.**

The four "Hebrew" brothers, were only obeying their Lord, no matter what evil *Satan* tried to work through legislation and *law of* the *land; - (*see Psalm 94:20*.)*

(What we thought, was - *"powerful":*
[and in which it was]; {very powerful).

-

(*Was only them, being* very *serious about keeping the LORD's* **commandment***s; and not breaking The Lord* (**YAH***'s) law: [(EVEN if it costed them Their Lives.)]* (*And – that's the part that IS Powerful, on their part!*)

Did you know the mark of the beast, will be in law.(?)
(Ut-oh!)

You law 'abiding-citizens', better quickly figure out, which law is best for you to **'abide'** *by.!*
But "as for me and my house": (the 'band', and *company of the prophets'), [we will boldly]* tell you, what the *law of the* LORD, is: and, it looks, *[well], sounds, 'like this'..*

ISAIAH 30

ISAIAH 30:20 –21 KJV

<u>20</u> And though the Lord give you the bread of adversity, and the water of affliction, yet shall not thy teachers be removed into a corner any more, but thine eyes shall see thy teachers: '

21 And thine ears shall hear a word behind thee, saying, **This is the way**, walk ye in it, when ye turn to the right hand, and when ye turn to the left.

*V*s. (22 – 23) **Says**:

22 Ye shall defile also the covering of thy graven images of silver, and the ornament of thy molten images of gold: thou shalt cast them away as a menstruous cloth; thou shalt say unto it, Get thee hence.

23 **Then** shall he give the rain of thy seed, that thou shalt sow the ground withal; and bread of the increase of the earth, and it shall be fat and plenteous: in that day shall thy cattle feed in large pastures.

THE officer's job IS TO TELL YOU TO COME out OF SIN, and back into the standard: [Because, there is one.. .

And why is this role (so important, for you, - (to have us?)

We are the officer's - of *the Law*,
reporting for duty.

-

Follow me, to the Office of The Prophet.

CHAPTER 2:
FALSE FALSE-PROPHET's

CHAPTER **Two:** *(2)*
False *F*alse-Prophets

(Here We Go.)

*As much as we could have a field-day talking about what "False prophets" are, I would like to **dedicate** this section to another matter: [about] what you think (is)*
– but **isn't!**
<u>Besides</u>: *I believe we have ample material out there from other viable sources, about the topic in 'that' regard. (Unfortunately, not – 'As' much as we think however, because "This <u>Document</u>" is about to nullify [some] of (those teachings.)*

-

In '<u>*THIS MUST BE DOCUMENTED*</u>' (*T.M.B.D.*), our story began *in the* INTRO *Section.* (We were on a "train," remember.)

    It was a much smoother ride - than the one you're taking and about to embark upon. (**I am not writing *this book***) *like the last one,* (in other words.)

So, this time, (in our imagination) **let'**s *think of a Plane.* (And planes and ***tracks*** have different perimeters.)

    It's about to get rocky, into our *climb.*

Prepare for take-off! But prepare for turbulence, *on the way* **there!**

    <u>We've got to **do** some serious *damage* **control** for the Kingdom *of* YAH'*s* Heaven,</u> (here on earth).

-

So, permit me to **Correct.**

Often, we are told, if a prophecy does not *'come to pass'*, it is a false prophecy / or better-yet, coming from a 'False Prophet'.
- That is ***not*** the example in the BIBLE.
- Nor walked out before *biblical prophets.*

I know that this doesn't 'sound' right, correct? But let me walk you through it, and "correct" this erroneous *thinking*.
– [watch-this.]

This again, is because we don't know what the actual function *is* for 'the prophet': but with **YAH**'s help. Let's find out!

First:
As I made mention *several times* at this point.
(Not knowing what a prophet is, is detrimental.)

Earlier, [in CP:1], I briefly brought up, that if you prophesy *houses* and cars, or to, 'individual – prophecies' (regularly), you are most certainly *operating* from the *'gift of Prophecy'*.
(One of the <u>nine</u> (9) <u>gifts of the *Spirit*</u>.) Gifted by the Holy Ghost.

DETOUR *(one).*
Everything I'm about to say for the next (several) pages are a sidebar,
and not *(the focal point) of this chapter yet.* But (*We'll get there.*)
Please keep that in mind: I'll even tell you when we get to the main idea.

-

I Corinthians 12:4-7 (8-10), (*11*), (The nine ***gifts*** of the Spirit.)
- *Not to be confused with* the *"function"*.
– (Jesus) ***John 14; & 16;*** KJV, tells us **Who** the Holy Ghost "is", -in- *what* He does.
– *(Paul)* ***1 Cor.*** tells us the *attributes* that *come*-along 'with'.

Not to be confused!

He **is** the **power** to walk upright: the (*'Person'* of the Holy Ghost).
"*after that the Holy Ghost has come upon you:*" - [Acts 1:8].
That **"power"**, (is for *'live-right'*), not for *'tongues.'*

So, Paul tells us what "*diversities*", "*administrations*" *and*
"*operations*" come *'along'* with having him *(come upon)* us does.

(*Also, reference: 1 Peter 1:2; John 14:17 (KJV)*
- Our 'Sanctifier'– (*'with'* us).
- * '*after*'-wards* [He], – (*in* us!)

He (hangs) *'around'* to cleanse: - make "room:"
 – and **after**, He comes *(in)*:
(-we call that 'sanctification'!)
- To get the 'junk' out, so **he** can come and (live inside).
 – The (tabernacle of YAH). (Rev. 21:3); *c.f.* (1 Cor. 6:19)

(Jesus) tells Us what Having *'Him'*, – (not '**it**'),
[John **14**:16, 26; **16**:13] - (*The Spirit of Truth), – is for.*

So, again, the nine Gifts of the *Spirit;* displayed, in [1 Cor.
12:4], are the attributes of His presence. *But "His* person", is to
give you **power** with Christ *to* **walk** *as* a **son**, or *daughter, – after*
becoming one, *in (St John 1:12),* in this wicked world.
- "When" *He* comes, He offers you **gifts.**
- *His* character leads you "*in all truth*". – [John 16].

But *we,* (the Church *essentially*) have told *Him* we want His gifts,
but (that) we don't won't Him.
 Because (if I wanted *Him*),
 - I can prophesy, (A*nd*) I can Still *Live Right*:
 (Because: that's what *HIM* does.)
 -

BUT – These examples I set before you, (about gifts), are tell-*tell* signs, you are operating in the function of – the "gift" of prophecy. (As one example:)

And <u>before</u> we get to the main focal **point** of why this chapter is called *False False-Prophet's;* I want to take *at least* one *other* <u>detour</u> and discuss briefly with you, about another aspect that many of us don't talk about:

[We'll call *This*]

True – & – false. *(Detour 2)*

What about the ones which are sharply operating in the *gift of prophecy*, (*One*, of the nine gifts of the Spirit), (which anyone can have access, if YAH **"gives"**. But can we be honest and deal with this: (?) -

The ones carrying titles as **"prophet"***; who have only been operating in the gift, are* **by definition – "false-prophets" too!** –

Not from the aspect that they are the adversary; deceiving, or beguiling, - or any *of* such, (and) *It's not even their own faults*), but because their Pastors ascribed it to them; (ordinations, and "confirmations"), that Heaven didn't Evaluate, nor recorded for them to be. All Because we haven't been **taught**: (and it is in humility when *I say this)*:

It is **not** common knowledge in the body of Christ, what a prophet "is". And, again, I say: *meanwhile*, the 'prophet's', go overlooked, in the back of the church.

<u>Prophets.</u> <u>Hear</u> <u>me</u>; (and hear me, clear).

Prophets of the Bible didn't prophesy at the drop of a dime, (although we can). But if – so, [that's the *gift*, not **the** – *prophet'*. All <u>prophets</u> went in pre-loaded with 'go and tell My people'; 'go tell Pharoah'; 'go to Nineveh, (cry and decree), and <u>say</u>.'

(I'll give you *scripture*, later.)
Go *to* - and tell them - 'this'- *(and the prophet)* *'verbatim'*
tells the recipient what they already know (going in), what
they are going to say [when they get there]. - It is already
downloaded: [that**'s the prophet in** 'operation']: *Part* **of** it.
- - -   -   - - -

(And when you get a true download from the LORD to go
on assignment as a *prophet*, that word stays on display in your
psyche (spirit), like a 'favorite' record, [*on repeat*], until you have
done the work, or released it. – (even if what you're *"hearing"*,
(and saying), is not so *'favor'-able.*
• That's **first!**

• **Secondly**:
      – It's time we get educated, (let the 'ordination'
      'prophets', (who are not) – turn their *licenses* <u>in</u>.

Make way for Prophets *to take* their place, *properly*, (**We** MUST).
  By us *finally* knowing what a-prophet *is*: [and **their** function].
  (While the Gift of prophecy still functions. (That's fine.)

     As long as the **church** can tell, *What's What.*
•   **It** is imperative *in the* (**end**) *day.*
     To (*respect the function* of the true prophet.)

(That's why the church, is hurting: 'real bad'), because of
that lacking! Because the prophets aren't functioning], nor are
they "recognized" for who [they] are - 'to' function.!
    MEANWHILE, (as I stated before): someone who has not
been called by HaYahweh to be a "Prophet", (is) walking around
with your prophet's – "badge".
    - (*officer of the* (**law**) •of *the Lord.*)

When we get that, the Church can get balanced:
> Proverbs 11:1 – (again:)
> *"A false balance is abomination to the LORD:*
> *but a just weight is His delight."*
> **# - Order in the court!**

If Paul said *(Ephesians 4:12)*; the' five'-fold ministry, is 'for the perfecting of the saints', and Father-**YAH** gave these administrations: all *five of them*: (this is not an indictment against those with the "gift" of / *to prophesy*).. But until the five-fold "PRO•PHET" takes his place *we* will never be "perfected", (and it's not about the prophet being *'special'*: - It's about all components **essentially** being present, utilized, and respected. - That's it.!

— '<u>al</u>l hands on deck.'

If our case were in the 21st-century church, that there were room for the *apostle*: *prophet*: *teacher*: and *pastor*.
And we left out **Evangelist**; *(for instance);* the church still would *be unbalanced* **&** *un*perfected. –
(*We're talking about* (the **real** operation) *Evangelist.*)

Let me show you what our YHWH showed me while we're on this subject matter, really (quickly), of [**The Evangelist**.]

Just for a moment –

True – & – false. II. [Detour *3*], *Final detour:.*
In the 21st and (20th, back then), *century* church: -too, particularly for the 'black - church' I have this observation: [which I *hate* that term], but I also have not been a watcher in a plethora of other's either. - But what I'm about to say is not based on *observation*, either way: but *'revelation', the LORD 'showed'* me.

In 2025, what the FATHER showed me concerning the evangelist, is that we're not raising up real evangelist, either:
 - *that* some people who have the title of "Evangelist" are not Evangelist), but they are 'ordained', from this perspective:
(*Their pastors knew that there was a 'calling' on the individual's life, – that they were 'called'; but they weren't quite spiritually mature enough to take on the role of an **Elder**, perse:*
So, (most) modern-day evangelists. (Their ordinations are as such), as a **place-holder**- A [(*misdiagnosis* again)], until they can 'grow-up.', (in the gospel!)

The "Evangelist" – ordination for most people, in the modern church is their '*holding cell*', (**the LORD showed me**). Until *or, should they* become 'mature' enough to become ordained *elders*!

(The church -functionally, is jacked up, a little bit; [respectfully]. Not *"the church"*, Jesus instituted. But what we made it out to be.

We have, or we've got "false evangelists",
 ➢ (*Not because they are Satan's*).
And "false prophets",
 ➢ (*Not because they are the devil's seed*). (***John** 8:44.*)
But *false, <u>in the sense</u>:* they are not in their rightful places: Misdiagnosed by spiritual leaders being irresponsible over these *ordinations*, (not knowing what they are ordaining people (*to*). Respectfully- again, I tell you.

(*I* Tim. 1:7,8)
[7] Desiring to be teachers of the law; understanding neither what they say, nor whereof they **affirm**.
[8] But we know that the law is good, if a man use it **lawfully**;

-

*And <u>we</u> ALREADY know about the leaders who ordain
'Evangelist's', because it's gender specific to them:*
-    *And that's not right, [either!]*

(Women, who are much more in-YHWH, *but are held there in a
prison cell, ("Evangelist"); only / [all]* because, *they are women.*
-        *Traditions of men.* [Mark 7:8] – *Not biblical standard.*

<u>**NOW**</u> <u>*for*</u> <u>*the*</u> <u>*real*</u> <u>*reason*</u> <u>*this*</u> <u>*chapter*</u> <u>*is*</u> <u>*called*</u>**:**
<u>*"False false-prophets"*</u>.
~ • ~

MISCONCEPTIONS

Often-times, (We Have cast out, refused, spoke bad, ex-
communicated, and "said" that they were 'false', (to those who are
fully authentic), *because of a misunderstanding of the prophet
(and his work).*

We all know the scripture, (1 Samuel 3:19)
*"And Samuel grew, and the LORD was with him,
and did let none of his words fall to the ground."*

And we base – (the bulk of our understanding) upon this:
of how to "prove" what a prophet (is) or if they're *authentic.*
That "alone", would be a false (balance) of this ascension
operation: -

But we also know that *a false balance is an abomination. –
[Pro. 11:1* KJV.]

Speaking of this:
(There are prophets of YAH. – And then, there are prophets
of Christ: (meaning, some are of the five-fold "prophet"

calling, *(like I mentioned, with the lady we started off with).*
And some of us, are old-school, natural-born prophets from
the womb. -
(Still through *Christ* however*: ascribed as Term, 'Seers'.)*

-

I won't say, I was 'conflicted', *(because "I" knew I was a*
(prophet). But when I was in my adulthood-younger years: I had at
least two encounters where separate pastors *at church's we were*
visiting, said to me: 'I don't know if you're a prophet, or an
apostle, but you're one of them.' – (1 *of* the 2.)

One encounter; early *twenties:* the other; 'early' *thirties,* ironically.
I was *conflicted* of (apostleship): **1.)** Because I *'didn't'* know what
an apostle *is,* in terms of its function. **2.)** I knew the Lord said to
me, the word beginning with the letter "(p)", - *(at. 18.)* So, I
always brushed *apostleship,* off*:* I was proud to be a prophet, so it
made it easy to *do so*: (I thought it a *great* honor!) • Still do.
(Just not so zealous. And I'm more seasoned, to understand the
responsibility is too great to be "pumped" and excited, rather
*than to shake with *fear*– [For whether you know it or not, a*
prophet's obedience, [lack thereof] *can cost their **life/salvation**]*
  • [***If I tell* you to** *tell* **the wicked man** *(he will die),* **and you**
  don't tell him: I'M going to hand out to you a punishment,
    equivalent to his. (says *the LORD*), - [*Ezekiel* cp. 3.]
❖ (***Cp.14:9***), - *too,* for another reference.
    V.10 • says "the *punishment of the prophet shall be even as. "*

Back then, I didn't understand, but now as I'm older *(in*
faith) and with my *journey*: I now know why the pastors couldn't
decipher, *which* one I was! – (I was 'both'.)
    (Feb. 2022), **THE SPIRIT** of Christ "said" to me: that I am:
– *"**a old testament prophet. AND a new covenant apostle.**"*

And then, He gave me a *shortened way* to say *or (to interpret)* **it**, which is where I adopted *this* and coined **the encounter** from HIM – [.]

"*Prophet of GOD: Apostle of Christ.*"

(He knew I didn't have 'conviction' for the term *"YAH"* back then, yet, so, **He** met me *right there_* and used the term '*God*' *concerning HIMSELF* when **He** spoke it to me. (**Then.**) (This was *nearly 20 years* after my **first** encounter I had in *the* church setting with who told me *they couldn't decipher for* me '*which*', I was; - a '*prophet*', or '*apostle:*')

- Meaning: my five-fold, ascension gift, is <u>apostle</u>: but I am an actual, real-life prophet: (like the ones), [watch this]: we "(**read**)" <u>*from*</u>, - &- <u>*about*</u> in the scriptures. ('*Introduction*' reference.).

OFFICER (*Cont.*)

An officer can show up to your doorstep, to enact a court's decree: to tell you of a penalty, although they are not authorized to fully give you the **final** verdict: though, sometimes, they can pronounce it. – "Court" <u>proceedings</u> still must go on: and for the *JUDGE*; for *Him* to make His ruling, - as *King*!

(And because "*we have an advocate with the Father, Jesus Christ the righteous:*" (**1 John. 2:1**), - Things can change...

Though A prophet, serve*s* (in the moment), as 'face' of the court – [they themselves are not the court, in itself; #*thingscanchange*, - But doesn't negate (that Prophets) are most certainly, a "part" of the infrastructure: [servants *of* the *court:* "ruling*";* - "order*";* - "instruction*:"* "(authority):".

-

[Think, **(*Ezekiel 3*)**. *Think* (Ezekiel 18), for extra measure.] The same way it is with **natural** *law*: the same it is with prophets!

An *Officer* can tell you you're being 'arrested' for a certain **charge**. (But you show up to court and *Judge* becomes merciful and give-s *to you* another verdict: or throw out all charges altogether, (Thank You Jesus, <u>literally</u>.) If you need proof of (this), please refer to:

-    *2 KINGS 20*
-    (ISAIAH 38:1)

(Referring *to* Hezekiah, [*king*]; Isaiah, (*prophet*).

"In those days was Hezekiah sick unto death. And Isaiah the prophet the son of Amoz came unto him, and said unto him, *Thus saith the LORD*, Set thine house in order: for thou shalt die, and not live." – /(This is scriptural), *meaning*, (documented).

2 Kings 20; Isaiah38, *starts* as the same record.

- Remember; an ***arrest***, is not the same as a **conviction**.

(But let us ***not*** mess with the *Most High* and find-out: *[that]* ***convictions*** do happen). - LORD *help us!*

When Jesus shows up in ***Revelation*** *chapter* **2/3** concerning the seven churches, He says to *5* of the *sum*: *'here are your **charges**'*, but (*with them*) - were *a* chance for repenting, – "<u>or, else</u>". and (*he says),* or "I come quickly", then *'remove your candlestick'.:*

(Therein is the *"conviction"* on display of what (could be), (*spoken verbally) (of)* '***if*** you don't *follow* the (*following*), **the Lord** *says!* – That's instruct-*ion*s.

❖   So, I say to you, *prophets* are instruct-*or*-s – *for* Him:

❖   He; *Convicting* of the ***royal*** court:

(Jesus does pass out death sentences.)

He says, "I will remove." • *LORD* help the church.

-

The work of the prophet, (nor it's Fruit), is for "accuracy". The work of the prophet, is for c/o/r/r/e/c/t/i/o/n: He sends (us) so He does ***not*** have to (send *His wrath*.) The **work** of the **prophet**, is to get you to know what the LORD, is *(about)* to do. –

Prophets of *The Most High* are your *'grace period'* showing up, - in hopes that you *"turn"*, so that **YAH** Doesn't **Do**: what He has pronounced He'll do.

(2 Peter 3:9)

"The Lord is *not slack concerning his promise, as some men count slackness; but is <u>longsuffering</u> to us-ward, not willing that <u>any</u> <u>**should perish**</u>, but that all should come to repentance*."

-

[Now; let's talk about *this*] – '(arrest)'.
= Spiritually used: what we say /*the* (**church** *[version]* term) is; *what **you think** of* when 'you' say *'conviction'*.

(LET'S FIX THAT)

In the court, a word that civilians use, has a completely different meaning: (In the court of **law**) * And in the court system, *down here on* Earth, it is often referred to as *'Legalese'*.
A true "conviction", means, A Verdict: = (*Final* Decision).
We are not 'convicted' (yet) (*literally*) when we feel shame *for our* sins.

We are (Arrested) by *His* Spirit; (**or** our Conscious in *most* cases, *'through'* **the *word***: because it lives in your "conscious:" – (Galatians 3:22–24), our "*school master*".
(***John 8***:*7-9*) – "*⁷ So when they continued asking him, he lifted up himself, and said unto them, He that is without sin among you, let him first cast a stone at her. ⁸ And again he stooped down, and wrote on the ground. ⁹ And they which heard it, being convicted by <u>their</u> <u>own</u> <u>**conscious**</u>, went out one by one, beginning at the eldest, even unto the last: and Jesus was left alone, and the woman standing in the midst.*"

- *The conscious,* is to know what's *right:* but *the word of YAH;* our *school master, helps us to discern it.*

❖ And 'we' call (that), conviction! – *It* is **not**!

(*Not* in the court of Heaven)'s *system*:

It's an *arrest*:

When you are stopped by the "police" (when *traveling*), it slows you down: *ironically from the hurry you were probably in; to get* to wherever you're/you were trying to get to: s*lowing down the process of* <u>the</u> ***direction*** <u>you're</u> <u>going</u> <u>in</u>. (* <u>catch</u> <u>that</u>: *)

AND
- Some people; just start back "speeding:"
- (While others, *[for some];* that ticket / **arrest,** causes (you) / them, to *'slow down'*, reflect, *and become more* <u>*conscious,*</u> *after they were 'stopped'.*
- *More "conscious" and reverend - to* (the **Law**).

BUT: (if one Doesn't turn), *'reflect'* - [Repent]..

[**Revelation 2:5**]. "*Remember therefore from whence thou art fallen, and repent, and do the first works;* **or else** *I will come* unto thee *quickly,* and will <u>*remove*</u> <u>*thy*</u> <u>*candlestick*</u> out of his place, <u>***except***</u> *thou repent.* " – , *"or"* ("else ") (be)*comes* the finality.:

(The legal term *'conviction'*, = *verdict,* / **guilty**.)

Thank You, JESUS. By the Blood of Jesus, *we* overcome:

—

PROPHETs
- WE ARREST.
- YAH Gives the *VERDICT*. – *(Final.)*

(Even, if He said something else, Before.

(AGAIN: think Isaiah; with *King* Hezekiah:).

[We're just getting started: This is not isolated: this is the work.]

(A repeat cycle amongst His. *(The LORD's prophets.)*

Memory Lane

I Remember there was a guy friend, that the Lord put me in proximity to. And how I met him was *(by another Apostle (buddy) of mine's invite* to this particular-individual's church, for a *Night Service* of a special kind that *they were having there.* And the night I met him, it was an immediate interruption of both our lives, [for certain!] - {[I say that with a chuckle in my spirit, but this was nothing short of serious]}. [For note also, the "apostle friend", who invited me; I didn't know all too well: *we had met shortly before, when I was scouting for a building to lease during that time for our church's ministry, and he worked in leasing*: (We met, we talked, expounded, and he even bought a copy of my first book, 'TMBD' (2nd EDITION), on the first day we met: *(Back to the night, at-hand:*). But that's who invited me to the *'other'* apostle's church - that we're getting ready to discuss: (and my engagement with *him*.)

I was walking heavily in consecration during that time: (Not meaning a *"fast";* but a lifestyle of 'constant', before *YAH*.)

While the pastor *(whose church, we were at),* was operating and flowing in his "gift", he got happy and came to *the back* where I was sitting and prophesied: (and that was fine.)

What you must understand, this person is my friend, and I love him [to this day], but 1)., we were strangers at the time, (which really doesn't matter), And 2), (an anointed man of 'GOD', he is). But he was living comfortably in his 'gift' being in operation, (but not his *hands being* clean *during **that** time*, and there was an area for him to 'clean' up.)

So, he prophesied to me: (that was fine), like I said before: but then - he put his hands on me. (<u>And the anger of the LORD,</u>

<u>was kindled.</u>) Ut-oh (wow). Not my anger, because I had to (wait) to discern fully, until the Father revealed it to me: It was not my anger - *again, I say to you* - confused for the anger of *YHWH*! (*Another man of YHWH prophesied to me too, (prior), during the night service, but he spoke from a 'distance', - (it might've been a church anniversary, as the occasion - or revival,* but he *stayed where he was,* up front: Then, it happened!

[There comes the 'man of God', whose church we were at, flaunting his "gift", - but walked up on a consecrated man who's living holy for real. And put their filth of hands *(by lifestyle),* on an anointed vessel:

That's when YAH's *A*nger was kindled against him… (Now, we're both his sons, yes - and - I'm no better than him), no.)

But somebody put their hands, who was in compromise during 'that' time, on a consecrated man of YAH, who's also a prophet. (YAH, got hot with him), Because,

(* And in all honesty, *in hindsight*, it was a setup. *)

THE LORD set me up to go attend that service that night, (because I barely go anywhere); ever: but - because *He* wanted to get the attention of 'another' son, who was not walking right. (But a son to YAH, nevertheless, *indeed.*)

So, as the days passed by, and now, our being in contact with communication, since we exchanged phone numbers, that night of the *service*: (We even, hung out, once or twice; but; it was all a "setup", **from Yah***:* of the Most High, to get me in close proximity to him:

The LORD told me to say (tell him "I'm going to kill him".) (I pondered, I prayed; I couldn't get it 'off of me'.)

–   Is he still living – yes, *thank YHVH.*
–   Was I *'a lying prophet?'*. – **No.** I wasn't.

(AND THIS IS WHERE THE CHURCH is confused.)

YAH, (by Christ: 'Jesus:') did just what the purpose was, "to get his attention", and tell him to stop playing with *His* people, (using his *gift*, and get consecrated (through holiness. -*or*- that *was* going to become his **verdict**: I wasn't a lying prophet. I told him what *YHVH,* said (I) *Say*: –and it yielded the fruit it was **supposed** to. (He repented; he cried out to *YHWH*.)

(I wasn't there, I wasn't in his closet, I know the fruit it yielded however, – that's how I know.) - Now, it's time I teach you what the LORD, (Most High), has taught me about being a prophet:

The *office of the prophet*, at its foundational level is what you must learn, (to be an adequate prophet, that teaches others how to discern <u>what</u>, is in operation! [It's your-time; to GUIDE The CHURCH, properly: it's time (you) get your "Badge", and walk in it: *[Hear this],*

> Remember, *in the* [book of the prophet], *(Jonah), and how he was sent to prophesy doom and destruction, from YAH?*
> By 'today's' standard, - (and this is me: saying this.) - <u>he</u> would be considered or called; *"a false prophet"*.

❖ *YHWH* Said to Jonah, 'go tell them, I'm going to kill them!'

[sidebar: **Ex. 22:24**: (YAH says: *"I will kill you"*, verbatim.) Because I know y'all *'think': 'He don't talk Like that!'* *(Hmmphf.)* [*c.f.*] – *Lamentation 2:21(KJV): – "killed"*.

Jonah said what *YHWH* told him to. - Jonah said: *'in 40 days this land / city* [Nineveh], *is going to be overtaken, and destroyed, and everybody, *in* it!* • [**Jonah 3:4.**]

'(Prophet)' Jonah was also angry that it didn't happen because it made him *look* like a ***false prophet***.! But the key here, is (and) what I want you to see, (is this):
Yah, 'could've' told Jonah – [hypothetically]; *'Go tell them people in* Nineveh, *IF* *they don't repent**, *I'M Going to destroy them.!'*

—

YAH in H*IS* INFINITE WISDOM knew that wouldn't be enough: He knew that if HE left "**if**" on the table, they would have thought they had more time, or -better-yet, *(for worse),* - had not taken the decree seriously: / *ECCLESIASTES 8:11 (KJV)*

- *"Because **sentence** against an evil work is not executed speedily, therefore the heart of the sons of men is fully set in them to do evil."* /

(that's literally what the Bible says: *King James Version:*.)
– read for further context.)

YaH can't trust us with *"if "*; because we '**play**.'!

So because, when (the LORD) sends One of HIS <u>Officers</u>, He sends us in; no sugarcoating, and *just* to deliver to them the final verdict, - without giving to *said* person, the room to "think" (they got more time), (because <u>**if**</u> you don't *find* true-repentance: the "verdict" that the (true) prophet-of- Yah, went and told you /would/ happen, - <u>will</u> come to Pass. (Without a doubt!)

-

This *is a conversation THE MOST HIGH* is *having with His (Prophet)-Jeremiah: revealing to us what the <u>work</u> and <u>fruit</u> bearing; (in his assignment of "a" prophet) is; -* in *<u>action</u>:*
(WHAT IT PRODUCES.)
(JEREMIAH 23)

"But if they had stood in my counsel, and had caused my people to hear my words, then they should have **turned** them from their evil way, and from the evil of their doings.**"**- (Jer. 23:22.)

ESAIAS/Isaiah delivered to king Hezekiah, the "final" "verdict", without telling him; (another hypothetical) here, (as if, I'm speaking for *Prophet Isaiah*, this time - as he went in, (on behalf of the Most High), to King Hezekiah (Hypothetically)*Speaking*: -

('*The Lord* SAID':

"-I've *decided* I'm Going to kill you: *but if you turn your face to the wall, Cry out, I'll hear you, – and I'LL change My MIND.-)*"

– Yah didn't [say] all of that, but isn't that **exactly** what happened?

Was *the LORD shortsighted*? -No-, He knew *(Eccl 8:11)*, - (If*) He* gave him all *(of)* that, Hezekiah wouldn't had taken - as serious: -But it *was serious*, and **time** was of the essence: (YAH doesn't have time for us, to continue in the **direction**; because we think we got options: Just tell them what the ultimate is going to be: and let's [see what they're going to do with that information: - [y'all understanding, the ['operation'?] _ "GOD", is literally, about to "kill you"; (if He's sending the prophets to tell you that.) - But the purpose, is so that He Don't *do*:

- The Ball is in your court, (*to the* "recipient:")

And you misdiagnose *YHWH*'s Grace, (through their repentance), as if the prophet, *was fake:* – No – We*('ve)* got so much to Learn: -So-, a lot of people that y'all are calling *false prophets*, are not, while depending on the gift (of accuracy), as the rubric, or *'system'*, to determine if Said-someone is a "*real*", seer: **(JESUS, I'm helping somebody: and I thank you!)**

-Even soothsayers, (palm readers), *and the* like, know "how" to be accurate; That - doesn't make it "prophecy", nor the work of *YHWH*, -&- (the Backing: of Christ), or the work *unto the LORD*,

[Jer. 23:22], (*that the 'true': PROPHET In [operation], is operating* either!).

Wasn't there a lady, in [the Book of ACTS], *16:16*, (17) – "*possessed with a spirit of divination*", *who* used: "*soothsaying*", *that 'prophesied'* (using *that* term loosely), a/c/c/u/r/a/t/e/l/y: who told everybody that stood by, or was passing that way, that 'these men be of YAH',-'*who've come to show us the way of salvation:*' (Doesn't that sound like a "right" spirit:? She *is* telling the truth, (*accuracy*): - even talking about "salvation". (LORD **Almighty!**) #Soothsaying: - *(The spirit it was in - was far from YAH's.)*

- And ***This*** – is the system, to determine if someone is a prophet?! – *No*. (Not *so*) – I Did not come to *play*: Because ***He*** didn't [*send*] me *to*!

YOU MUST know (*The* function) of a prophet. To 'properly' gather- if One is, or ***not***!

(Oh My-Yah, I just said something!)

Prophet's correct! Not, tell ***accuracy***! (I'm not a soothsayer: I'm A Prophet: I didn't come to tell/(nor ***sell***) you "accuracy": I came to SHIFT you: (That's a PROPHET!)

(But let the word of *YAH* from The Lord, come to a prophet, concerning [warning], and one doesn't take heed or turn to repentance and *see* [how '*Accurate*' that prophet is!]

– (#*REAL- Prophets*).

You better hope their words are not accurate!

The '*(contingency)*' is on you. If you found the appeasement of *HAYAH,* [*H*e was looking for]!

- Doesn't make the prophet/nor the word he/*she* spoke, inaccurate: it just means, *you* **shifted** where you needed to be, so *it wouldn't come to pass;* because, after all: ***YAH*** desires, ***that no man should perish*** – [2 PET. 3:9]. – Him *(not)* making the prophet's-words, come to pass; were the INTENDED results *of the Most High,* to **begin** with. (Now, *you're* seeing: are you?)

- -

Jonah: was *upset*, because, if I could put it in my *own* words for just a minute; from him: he'd say something, as–such: (This is the way the scripture **describes** it from *the* way *in which* he was 'feeling': – (Another hypothetical): but not really (this actually happened: THIS Is more so; A play on words of what was taking place, going on, and happening at the scene: *[Jonah **4:1-4**]*.

" –Why wouldn't you just let me say, *If*?– "

" –Because: *YOU* got me out here Looking crazy.–
'(Now my credibility is on the Line, (with the *church*) [people]: and they're going to think I'm a 'false–prophet;'– "
" –BECAUSE WHAT I SAID / *(And "You" told me to say it).*
- DIDN'T come to pass:–)"

   - #upset:

When *YHWH* told me *to go to the apostle;* to go tell him what He said, *He* didn't grace me with *a* "if", as the Messenger, [nor the entail]. And [*MOST HIGH*], didn't grace the recipient with an "IF", either:

The LORD, (through Christ Jesus), told me to tell him: - "I'm going to kill you!" – And *that's* what I delivered.
*(and you better say it 'Like' - **He** told you).*
– *Moses can tell you:* Changing *His* Instructions, *can cost you –* '*your' Promise!* **#SaywhatHesaid:.**
– It wasn't easy, but I delivered it:

Those in immaturity, and don't know the ***function*** of the **(office)**, would've loved *as an opportunity* to, - make that - a "*false-prophet*' out of me: [the devil is a liar:].

A *'false prophet'* (Misdiagnosis.)

YAH is *so* merciful; *He*'ll always send out a *'warning shot'*. *(This is* not about calling *HIS* bluff because a true <u>shot</u> won't miss!) - *H*e has perfect aim: though sometimes when *He rounds off a "shot"*; (He doesn't let us know, whether; [*to* the *prophet* or *recipient*]; when and if: the {'bullet' in the chamber} is *a blank*. [Is that a risk you're willing to take]? – *Let's keep going*.)

- the Bible says: *"not willing, that any should perish"* –

YAH **is not a joke:** *He's just sending you warning, first.*

(Ezekiel. 18) says no matter what you've done; how wicked you've been, if you turn, I'll hear you. [There are some stipulations, - because some proclamations ARE Final]: - *that's* WHY we can't play with HIM. – It won't go well.

So, when I told my friend that YAH was going to kill him: *YAH* got the perfect results; (a win-win), and I wasn't a false-prophet. It yielded the precise results *YAH* intended it to: Even though *YHWH* didn't "tell" me He *didn't mean it*; **(see the semblance with JONAH;** *He didn't tell Jonah -* *"He didn't mean it")* **-** because *He* **did** ('mean' it), (in both cases): He just didn't tell us: *me,* [Jonah], or Isaiah. – *(I'm not trying boast myself with these mighty men:* I'm just trying to show you what the (work) of someone like me: who indeed is someone like them: {looks like!}. - So, you can correlate, what us prophets are doing: *PROVING* it to you *through* **the text,** (and the modern-day), the 'function' never changes! - No matter how many centuries, and generations pass, or *doth* go by: That's how "I" know some of you all (are) not. Because your (function) is telling on you: - It's okay: It's just that YAH, is a God of measure: and Order: - He's tired of us measuring something other than what He gave us: - It's time to respect, -

THE PROPHET: (The office: function; measurement: not so much, the *person*). But the person, is the person, 'God' chose; *the mighty YHWH*, for the office: I simply(*Put some respect on it!*)

-

- Court could *be* going on: And a 'trial' would commence:
- Heaven would meet with defendant, Remotely, **i.e., (prayer) – (*Jonah 3:5-9*):** Jesus show up, *our Advocate*, and he plead our cause with the-Prosecution = *(YHWH's decree).* (To determine if one is *weighing in the balance (**DAN. 5:27**):* determining the final judgement; verdict: - (absolute) **ruling.**

*[10]And Yah saw their works, that they turned from their evil way; and **Yah repented** of the evil, that **he** had **said** that he would do unto them; and he did it not.* - (Jonah 3:10: KJV).

"He said", – (not "the prophet said": And the MOST HIGH, HIMSELF, changed His MIND: does that make Him; "A-Lying-(false)-GOD"/? – I'm just asking(?)
- ❖ *So, when **He** does move from what **HE** said:*
- *it does not make the "Prophet – False"; either.*
YAH, chose (2 Pet. 3:9), (AND we thank HIM.) instead:

And I know, my friend found true repentance. Because he's here. We thank *YHWH*, HAYHWH:

JONAH

Jonah said, they all were going to 'die': but *"if my people" (2 Chr. 7:14)*, kicked in, and (due to their *'Repentance'*), the entire city was spared: ~ **That,** is the work of a prophet: (not – *Accuracy.*)

Accuracy has its place: but that is not the full scope of the working of *the **prophet**: (IT's Not Even the Main Objective).*

– (Quite contrary: If the intended purpose *[for **warning**]* = 'Redirection': *(and the <u>work</u> / <u>fruit</u> of the prophet –according to*

the LORD's office, is SHOWN in **(Jer. 23:22)**; then 'the Prophet's' ought to be *"accurate"*, – as **less** as possible.

We were sent to redirect: [traffic], not take you to *the* gas chamber, or *electric* chair:

*The **true** intentions, is Not to kill you: - Most High, YHWH: Is trying to do EVERYTHING He CAN: BEFORE walking up to your tree, and cursing it, Forever*: *See the [Fig-(fruit)-tree], here* **[MATTHEW 21:19]** = *#DEATH:*

v. 19b: - *"Let no fruit grow on thee henceforward for ever."*

Jesus does pass out (death) sentences:

v.19c.) - *"And presently the fig tree withered away."* (KJV).

This is **the work of the prophet**: - to bring correction…

Rather than <u>death</u>: - because that; (*concerning: **'warning'** in "operation"*); is <u>the other option</u>.

- To the *recipient: (Warning has* come *to.)*

AND <u>to</u> the prophet; because we don't want to just discuss *them:* ***Real*** FREE-WILL *for the* (Chosen) - *is 'Obey'; "-or- DIE:".* *'You not going to be bearing "figs" for the enemy: when I created you **(Jonah)***'*– [for you hard-headed folks]*– 'to bear fruits for Me:'. - - #ChooseyethisDAY.*

- *To* the *servant – "the prophet:"* (Amos 3:7.)
    - *The Sent Ones! (#Go.)*

Then, **Jonah** had *the nerve* to tell ***the LORD***, 'I knew You were going to be merciful: That's why I didn't go!' - (wow). – JONAH 4:2, - (KJV, *Paraphrased*).

-

In my heart, concerning *the guy THE MOST HIGH sent me to, (*I knew in my heart, He did not Desire 'to', but that He *would, if necessary: The Spirit of "the LORD" never told me "if"; but I did know it was for* Correction: *because the stipulation **YAH** gave* *to me was to wait until he got my first book, in *his hands:** (Because *in* that book, was the '(type)' of 'correction' he needed for his situation.) *So, by my knowing–that, I knew 'God' wanted to shift him, and (preserve) him: rather than -'actually' to 'kill him'.*

Depending on the contingency or the dependability upon if we respond, or if we heed: - *if* we should 'turn'; (meaning 'the apostle' *though,* in this instance.)

Listen to what THE *FATHER* gave me, *through Jesus Christ;* based-*from*: (*2 Chronicles*). The way *the LORD* has given it to me, to explain Himself **to** *you,* of the way He moves: *Watch this* - THE **LORD** *says:*

(2 Chronicles 7:14)
"If My People, which are called by My NAME *would humble themselves,* and Repent: *Then* **I** *will* REPENT, *of the former* [*Judgment*] [that] I Said [that] I would do." – (wow).

-

➢ **EZEKIEL** (KJV) **33**
Cross Reference, **(Ezek. Cp. 3; Cp. 18.)**

❖ ***EZEKIEL 33:*(5a/b), *7–9***
5 "He heard the sound of the trumpet, and took not <u>warning</u>; his blood shall be upon him."
5-b.) "But he that taketh <u>warning</u> shall deliver his soul."
-

7 "So thou, O son of man, I have set thee a [watchman] unto the house of Israel; therefore thou shalt hear the word at my mouth, and **warn** *them from* **me**.
8 When I say unto the wicked, O wicked man, thou shalt surely die; if thou dost not speak to <u>warn</u> the wicked from his way, that wicked man shall die in his iniquity; but his blood will I require at thine hand.

9 Nevertheless, if thou warn the wicked of his way to turn from it; if he do not turn from his way, he shall die in his iniquity; but thou hast delivered thy soul."

Chapter 3, Is an entire cross-ref: but let's *home in* on some.]
EZEKIEL 3:18*, 21*

[18] When I say unto the wicked, Thou shalt **surely** die; and thou givest him not **warning,** nor speakest to warn the wicked from his wicked way, ***to save his life***; the same wicked man shall die in his iniquity; but his blood will I require at thine hand. *Notice how* when YAH *says*, "When I [**say**] to the wicked person; they shall die:" –

❖ [Prophet], when you ***tell*** them, it is:
  "to save his life:" [?] - (You see the formula?)

- Now: where does *YHVH* say, (your *purpose*, or 'His' for sending you, was *for accuracy*)?
- *It's for:* **turning***; restoring: delivering (from' death): not to* **Produce** *it: - (Death) is the result of what they didn't do: and* (they) - *did* **not** *"turn": That was never the Purpose* **(though)***, - that they (should)/would die! Even, [in most cases If Most High] said they would, - THIS Is mercy showing up, because; He actually is: "about to kill you"; and the prophet (Saying it), is most-likely your Last chance to plead your Cause [Hezekiah]; and /* **or***: 'Get it right!', (if sin is in the camp, or* is the #issue for why He's saying it: - #thewickedman:

Prophet, -'GOD' isn't (studying) our Ego, to be right: (*accuracy*).
"Your job" *(Is)* = *Deliver* **them** *(From)* **death:**
(Not): *Everybody knowing:* **"*you*powerful"***, (as they say),*

= ***Because*** *your 'words' "(came to pass)", – that's not the work of the Prophet, [its fruit], nor the Heart (of) the "God" WHO Sent You:*

– *(Deon Williams).* *On* **behalf** *of the MOST HIGH.:*

[v.21] **²¹ Nevertheless if thou warn the righteous man, that the righteous sin not, and he doth not sin, he shall surely live, because he is <u>warned</u>; also thou hast delivered thy soul.**

Because ***he was warned***: (Even though *YHWH* said He would:*(die)*.
YHWH even SAID **"surely"; but if the recipient receive & heed the warning of** the prophet /& [turn], 'warning'; can *reverse* it! –

(**Now**.) We have better understanding of what happened *with* Hezekiah, the king; <u>*and*</u> his **Encounter** with the Prophet (Isaiah); (although, in this instance, scripture never confirmed or said that in Hezekiah's case it was for wickedness, or for sin: As a *matter of fact*; scripture never mentions, For what cause *YHVH'*s decree was to him, as such: because Hezekiah shows to have been living "right": (scripture *confirms* it)*; -* so, I can only assume, - His life was (used) *to show us, in modern-day:* what the work of the prophet looks – like: **Think,** ***from the perspective;*** (of) when "Jesus': let Lazarus: die: because, *He* was going to prove - (a greater glory), as an example to us: -and-; the man born blind, when Jesus said it was <u>**neither**</u> sins from the parents or this child who *had* "become of age", that sinned: (but for the specific purpose, for "***YAH-to get the glory***", (through his healing!) –
Maybe that's (**why**) we have this particular interaction between (King)Hezekiah, and *(the LORD of Host) because usually when He tells somebody they are about to die, it's (usually); for the reason of sin.* But for Hezekiah, *that was not the case, for him,*

*(and due to "sickness": [maybe this is more closely related to Lazarus' Case than we formally believed, or imagined: But Here's the real reason: **(seems** like:).*

*— Sometimes; when you walk closely with **the LORD**, He will grace you, with telling you when (your time is up!) Not sin, (due) [to]: - (just **communication**)!*

HEZEKIAH: (might not have been *"living in" (sin),* (at the moment)*, but his time was either "up", (AND THE LORD Wanted him to (KNOW). - Or; there was **something (that needed to be recalibrated),** (that **telling him**, he would 'die', would (fix).*
- Or a (couple) of other (plethora) of ways, as to why!
We Cannot we understand ("His ways")- are not like our own.

BUT Overall**: #theworkoftheprophet:** RIGHT here in our faces, (Of how this thing works), – All along:

"Go Back:" - '*I reconsidered*:'. [To Isaiah]:
I changed *My* MIND, (because) I Heard You: - - *[to the king],*

- *Your Righteousness was counted*: (Hezekiah). - *(Is. 38:2,3).*

  —

- *Your repentance is accepted*, (wicked man). - *(Ez. 18:21).*

This is the work of the prophet:
THE (office) of Correction.

Regressing,

CHAPTER 3

The OFFICE of CORRECTION

CHAPTER **Three:** (*3*)
The Office of Correction

When speaking of the terminology, *the* 'office of correction': –
we're always referring to, "The Office of a PROPHET."

    Now: I'll tell you what "Correcting", really Is.
-   So, *first: I'll put it into words.*
-   *Then, display the* **action**, *(with my words).*
  1. (What it is.)
  2. (How it applies.)

    In order to do that, (I have to *begin by* wrapping up the
conversation that was *had* between me and *YHWH*), *I promised I*
would *give you earlier in the opening Chapter.*

\-

    In 1998/'99, at the "age" <u>18</u> years old: **the Lord** (said) –
I've Called you into the office of *a* **prophet.**

    And this is how that **conversation** went.

And "here", - was wisdom He placed *in* me to *ask the following.*:

I asked the LORD, (<u>what does a prophet's do</u>)? –
(See:-it was good that He kept me away from what we see in today's time, (and from the ***prophetic houses*** *I was wanting to be in* back then, *or a part of - that I told you about also* (in the 1ˢᵗ cp.) *Because had*-**He**, - I would have *automatically* thought, I ***knew***.
  – "What a prophet 'do'!"
I said: *(and these were my words, as I remember them Precisely.)* - Here was "His" wisdom (once again: worked through me in this moment, - but the innocency of a-child (*18*), worked in my favor!! - Not thinking *that* I'm knowing, - I ***asked*** and *said* – "What is a prophet (for)?" - or '**do**'. First, as I said: - <u>Then I said</u> –

<u>"I know a prophet don't just go around prophesying to people.!?"</u>
  And the *LORD* said to me:

"A prophet is called to bring correction."

(Just like *that).*   -   As clear as day:
[This set my life up, properly!]
Somebody *is about to get their AHA moment:*
Or is getting it - right now! (*Why you are, the **way** you are.*)

THIS BOOK is the work of [the prophet], itself: - And *I'm not speaking, singular,* **Deon Williams**, I'm speaking - the *function:* 'operation' of the *prophet*, in itself, no matter who/se name was attached to it. (Prophet's, "correct".)

THE *"PROPHET"* is working:.. on these pages, (and each, as they may), <u>'CORRECTION'</u>.: [this **book** is the work of 'the prophet' in operation, [right now]: - [Lord] *Jesus.*

(And this began my journey into the lifestyle and Official training
of being a prophet of the true and living God / YHWH.)

—

Basic Training

Often, when we hear of correcting; we think of it in only (one)
way: We'll **begin** there, then explore some other ways that *this*
applies.

(BUT FIRST)

❖ *Prophetic Training (Prophet's edition:).*

All ministerial/leadership 'callings', makes you an ***officer*** of
something: but the office of the prophet, has a higher clearance:
that's why we are trusted to change governments, (through)
"kings", govt's, - (but, by way *[of prayer] – and our mouthpiece).*
But why also our warfare is deeper: because "principalities", are
assigned (against) us:
- Sometimes, prophet's warfare is so deep, you may think they are
lazy or unmotivated, because they don't acquire a lot of 'things' as
(often) that other people do, - but you are unaware that one of the
ways the enemy; Satan, *the devil,* fights prophet's, is through the
spirit *of 'Sabotage'.*

 – **IF you don't believe this to be true,** *look at the life of*
Joseph*; of Daniel: Hananiah, Azariah, and Mishael, (The*
"Hebrews.") - Look at the life of **David***:* (All these *men,* being
prophets) or *seers.* (And yes, David was *a* prophet - Acts 2:29, 30).
(Sabotage was the "weapon" - that did *form, but it didn't* prosper.)

 - *'A Principality'!*

 (*Understanding this to be a 'spirit',* working *through* these
"men"), (**against** *these*)

 When they both were *babies:*

- Herod (king) – Tried to sabotage – ***Jesus****.*
- Pharoah (king) – Tried to sabotage *Moses.*

 – *'**P**rophets'.*

Which, 'babies' also speaks to the origin of "*this*" (conversation) I'm Having with you: back *in* [cp 1], when we 'discussed' if you are a prophet; you came through the womb, [that way]. And whenever YAHWEH (told you), was just *time* for you to know: *"not when you became."* - Remember that**!?** -

—   • • • • • • • • • •   —

King James Version Holy BIBLE (KJVA) 1611. –
II Esdras 5:48,49,51-54 (**Apocrypha.**)
[**48**] Then said he unto me, Even so have I given the **womb of** the **earth** to those that be sown in it in their times.
[**49**] For like as a young child may not bring forth the things that belong to the aged, even so have I disposed the world which I created.
[**51**] He answered me, and said, Ask a woman that beareth children, and she shall tell thee.
[**52**] Say unto her, Wherefore are unto they whom thou hast now brought forth like those that were before, but <u>less of stature</u>?
[**53**] And she shall answer thee, They that be born in the strength of **youth** are of one fashion, and <u>they</u> that are <u>born in the time of age,</u> when the <u>womb faileth,</u> <u>are otherwise.</u>
[**54**] Consider thou therefore also, how that ye are less of stature than those that were ***before* you**.

     – So anyway: Surely if these two men, being greater; (Jesus, *being* GREATEST), were not exempt from (sabotage 'attempting' them), then *surely*: we, *in this Generation, of a 'lesser stature'* - are not exempt from some weapons, forming, (and in some (*'small'*) cases, *prospering)! "Sabotage."* (Meaning
• *'gaining'* "an advantage".) (***2 Cor. 2:11***)

*- BUT as it pertains to the (**scripture itself**) the rest of the scripture*

(THIS MEANS When the EARTH *herself, was YOUNGER: She "GAVE Birth" to men of greater stature.*

** Our brains worked naturally better, - (with more "brain" power also, because there was (more oxygen:- as a–[sidebar.])*

• We're so prideful: and think we're so advanced: when we pale in comparison to the technology of the past: (oops, did I just say that?) - #BUILDMeAPyramid:
- And that's just (one example. - They (also) had 'electricity':
- We "ain't" doing (much of) nothing, compared to them: -

*They had wifi'D electricity, also: and the (**SUN is the** ether), that if you harness it, 'power' can go WHER-Ever the Sun shines on.)*

(Let's Move On.)

[THE RAINBOW *of* CORRECTION]

–

(Nitty Gritty:)

19 And Samuel grew, and the LORD was with him, and did let none of his words fall to the ground. [**1 Samuel 3**] (KJV)
20 *And all Israel from Dan even to Beersheba knew that Samuel was established to be a prophet of the LORD.*

[I don't say this disrespectfully towards the text, [<u>but</u>] *this has been the same spiel 'we've' used throughout the years to determine, [if] one is not, or [is]: 'a' prophet!*
– And We often hear: 'to root out'; 'tear down'; etc.:
with no explanation of that either: - Jeremiah. 1:10.

____

Often (Ascribing "accuracy", as our only contributor.)

–

(Now) **When we think of** *Correcting*, **we think of Nathan going unto David; telling him *he did something wrong*. –**

'Wrong' exists beyond the sphere, of human error. When we, as prophets, *were given power, we we***re give**n authority to bring 'things' <u>into *rightful* order</u>. - *(whatsoever* **the LORD** Says.)
- Correction*(s)*, exists outside of 'you' doing something.

So, when we think of correction, we like to think *on it; that way, of* (2. Sam 12). So, let's start there:

(The **list** include' • but is **not** *limited* **to** *the following.)*

The Rainbow of Correcting

"(VERBAL WARNING)"

(Ok, Here I'm going to weave *in* and *out* of a couple of things, (so bear with me: Starting with: - (***David*** & **Nathan**)

And the reason, I'm (doing a lot of ***"Corrective Detouring"***, is because there **is** 'a lot' **that needs to be** *CORRECTED* in the [body of **Christ**]: (I'm not even trying to do this, or make *myself* seem deep:
IT Is literary *the Holy Ghost* having me divulge all this information, - *as* **it** ***comes* up -.**

    o **(I would like to completely,** stay on 'topic':
But - - "To much, is given: much is required:"
(*St. Luke* **12**:*47*,**48**). –
v.47 • emphasis, on *"('**knew**' his lord's will)"*.
- Because I (know), I *('got')* - to tell you.

    • He's requiring that I give it to you.

– THE OTHER ***numerical*** LIST here will be without ('detouring'), so bear-through with me, to point No.1). Please.

– **Also p***ertaining to* THE OTHERs: - Points (2); (3); (4), etc., will be 'short, *but sweet*:'- (Straight to "the "point".)

(***David*** & **Nathan**) *(2 Samuel 12:2 –*
This is the type I just talked about that we're most use to:
(Also: a lot *of **what*** Cp. 2 Displayed.*)* • But <u>let's dive deeper</u>.

Now Speaking of • 'something **wrong**' (previous page). (Let's get this overall theme out of the way. So, I can dig into my other (points) without leaving out very (important) key factors.
(And I believe), there's no better place to address this, than right here: in the area section that's addressing **errors:** in human-form.)
Thus, in the *"Verbal Warning"* (section), here, we'll address a ***sub***

section, topic. ([which could stand on *its* own]), and then tie it all together SEE:*[P•T-2: Below:]*

– **In which,** *or by [doing **so**], or addressing this now, will be a grand theme, (because you need to know your **authority;** no matter what plethora* of 'OPERATION' you may be [functioning] in - in a moment: | And it just so happens, it [fits] better here, so let's get with it: *-then, (I won't have to continue in lengths after the /first point, of - 'Verbal Warning', because linking it here): (the tying together, should happen automatically., I'm sure hoping. And by the* **close** of this (sub): a lot will have been covered. [Strengthening the 'point' of the section, itself.]

[Chapter **3***: has been my most challenging, thus far.*]

-

- • ***Prophetic Training 2*** • **(Authority)** *Subtopic*:
  (To show you the function, and ***security clearance*** of a prophet, in ***YHWH****'s Kingdom(e) in* operation, as it pertains to when a prophet (IS) being sent to tell Someone, "they've done something, *'wrong'*. –
  (Or their authority, just in general:)

The Bible shows us, that prophets have the ability, power, and the authority; God-*given* of the Most High, to *rebuke* kings, - *(principalities), rulers, pastors;* [governmental infrastructures:] *churches, **etc**.*

See [*Dan. 9:6*]: *(*Ps. 105:14-15):*
And: [2 Sam. 12:1–7; (7b – 9, 10, 11-13).]; which is about – Nathan & David: and that we'll come to.

> *Jeremiah 1:10 (KJV) •* *"See, I have this day set thee*
> *over the nations and over the kingdoms, to root out,*
> *and to pull down, and to destroy, and to throw*
> *down, to build, and to plant."*

We often focus on the latter part of this verse, but let's go
'higher', as in; *to the **top** (of the verse).* And see what it says.

- (Jer. 1:10) – Says prophets are over what? You're right; you
  got it, <u>*nations*</u>**,** and <u>*kingdoms*</u>: (meaning to turn the heads,
  authority; - *of those who* bear rule: i.e., (kings.)
  - ***C.f.*** See: – [***Pro.21:1***.]

Look at *Daniel 4:27*, **"Wherefore, O <u>king</u>, let my <u>counsel</u> be**
acceptable unto thee, and <u>*break off thy sins*</u> by righteousness, <u>and</u>
<u>thine</u> <u>iniquities</u> by shewing mercy to the poor; if it may be a
lengthening of thy tranquillity.**"**

   - Rebuking the "king"; to repent!

*-*A Prophet*, told his king:* ['you need to *'come out of sin'*.]'

- Just as Nathan, rebuked the *king*, David; to whom/which had all
the rule of the kingdom: *[2 Sam. 12:1–14].*
The king[s]! - Who could've said, in *any* of these
circumstances; *(and there are multiple of them),*
- "off with [their] head*['s]*. "

            –

DID YOU KNOW: that David, was Nathan's dad:
Nathan (*the Prophet*); was (*king*) David's son !/? ! whoa: ?
Did you? (Nope; you didn't!) I highly doubt, because *it's*
cushioned in the scripture so **well** (Jesus showed it to me),

- St. Luke 3:31 (KJV) • N/T
- 2 Samuel 5:14 • O/T (KJV)

*To protect my credibility in the community of Theologians:
(and Over-all)..I'LL say: (potentially).:* **B***ecause 'some'
believe: this 'may' have been a different Nathan: than
David's - son.*

(According to scripture: David (could) be *Nathan's* dad.)

-

(Well: Someone may say, Nathan then, got *'away'* because: 'well,
then':. "it was his dad." – Nope, It was because of the authority /
[spiritual *Clearance*] that a prophet has, (has been *given*.) --(being
that <u>type</u> of **Officer**.)
  – Were Hezekiah(*king*); and Isaiah(*prophet*), related?
  – Were Joseph(*dreamer*); and Pharoah/(*king*), acquainted?
  – Were Daniel and Nebuchadnezzar "*pals*", when the Seer told
    (the king) YHWH would take his kingdom away from him? -
    [Those are 'fighting words, to a 'king'].

(What about Saul), when Samuel had to deliver to him, [the news]
his *kingdom* had been stripped away, (permanently) from him;
{unlike Nebuchadnezzar *who got his back at some point*}:
-    The list goes on and on.

—

But the prophet's told **kings**, what no one would dare say. We are
literally the mouth-piece of *YHWH*: - we-say, 'what He say'.

And; we go-in: knowing 'what' He 'say', (already) - before we get
there: **That's a prophet**, not that beautiful *thing* that everybody is
so impressed with: (*Giftings*).. *so let's discuss that a little further*:

- *Gift(s) of Prophecy.*

-You do know, when - *"the gifts and calling are without repentance"*, Is mentioned in (**Romans 11:29**); it's not talking about 'you' repenting, - BUT actually about Creator: (Wait, what!) **Yes• •YAH** *doesn't* 'repent' / (take back) 'the gift" once *He* gives it to you, - (Even when He 'finds out' you're 'misappropriating' it: *[That* is why witches and palm readers, can operate.*]*

- Because the Most High, YHWH doesn't snatch back the (gift). And because you can *prophesy, accurately, then* go *home ;get in the bed with another-man; to lie with him,* <u>*sexually*</u>. *[Lev. 18:22]:* (**because** *your Gift work: – is WHAT gets you in trouble:*
    [St Matt. 7:23:]
    [THIS MUST BE DOCUMENTED: (book) reference:
    (Go read, and go "get." –(shameless plug), because
YHWH wrote it, and it has much more information in it *than meets the eye*: It's <u>not</u> for the *LGBTQ+ only: it's for the* **entire body** *of CHRIST; - it might [help] you more than the lgbtq+d, (actually).*
[He has some other things to say to those who live outside *of that sphere, as well.] –* I PROMISE you. Most certainly!
        -

    But anyway. – **YAH** *doesn't take, /("repent" = take the gift back, just because you're using the gift without being clean (in your lifestyle), • He just lets you work it; get your reward from man. [Matt. 6:kjv reference]; - 'you have your reward' / (that's who you did it for); -their IMPRESSIONS, rather than for* <u>**Me**</u>*: [the LORD says]. Because "if you did it for Me"; according to scripture; the LORD says –*
    •   *you would: "keep my commandment'*, [Jh. 14:15] - that I [expect], and require of you:
    (Be holy, and *be* clean, with your gift.)

*And that's, <u>the</u> <u>thing</u> we're impressed with the most; 'gifts', (that work, **whether you acquire holiness**, or not).* Yikes!

And YAH doesn't "take back": - so that (can't) be the rubric we use to determine if someone is in "right STANDING:".
(Matthew 7:)

[22] Many will say to me in <u>that</u> <u>day</u>, Lord, Lord, have we not **prophesied in thy name? and in thy name** have **cast out devils? and in thy name done** many wonderful **works?**

[23] And then will **I** profess unto them, *I never knew you*: depart from me, ye that work iniquity.

-

*AGAIN, that's why YAH-got-hot with the apostle: [him putting his filthy hands on me (**during** that **time**);* (Sorry to say it that way.) But *(being impressed with his gift, but still not lined up in rightful "standing" with YHWH, in purity, -(When he decided he wanted to lay-hands on me.)* - That was not **"authorized"** by the kingdom of Heaven: and *that's why there's an emphasis on 'wanted', 'to'.*
- **Yah** told me to tell him:
- (I'm sending *my* wrath, to your breath.!)
Those were not *His* words (verbatim), (but we've already had *that* conversation; (Cp.2): *and* talked about that.)

'The CHURCH' is infatuated with prophecies; but despise *(the Prophet's).*
EVERYBody thinking' (themselves to be right in their (own eyes: *(Proverbs 21:2)*, - So, who wants to be corrected:**?**
Me – *(not that it feels good)* **but Here's what I** teach my congregation @SFIMATL *Ministries*), •
- ***"Correction is your best friend:"***
That's something the *Lord* laid on me, and here's a scripture too: PROVERBS 27:5,6, •

" **5**Open <u>rebuke</u> is better than secret love: **6** Faithful are the wombs of a friend; but the kisses of an enemy are deceitful."

    – And in my 20's - (early): (The **Lord** said to me: 'You not telling people the truth, (because you don't want to hurt their feelings', does more damage to them, than good:– (in the long run:)". **Then He** said to me: - *'YOU MAY BE THE ONLY PERSON, I (HAVE) to tell them the TRUTH', (meaning, of those in [their sphere]; (It may have even been an assignment for you. '*

(WATCH: This: Correlation.) (I just talked about prophets have to say hard things to "kings", *or those who are in leadership: - Don't misinterpret this: (but "she may 'be your friend': because* **the LORD** *is depending on you to tell her the truth – TO (HELP her). whoever *she* is.* (GOD placed you there to Be a REAL / TRUE *friend; (Pro. 27:5,6), That's the way. - Real (love) cuts it away, Cut the cancer out:*

    – *"[The first step to Recovery is admitting you have a Problem]" they say:. ("Scripture?", (you) say?, 'Because that's not 'Biblical'. – Well 'Sure':* Here It Is

        • *KJV [Romans. *10:17*],*
        *(And please review (**v.13.**).:. Very Important:*

*Faith come by hearing, and how can they apply, if they don't (first) hear it? - Somebody's soul salvation is {**locked up**) in the TRUTH* **you carry** *for them:* **Do you carry JESUS:?** *- Because He said:* **"I AM the truth.** [John 14:6]."

    (YAH is after (souls), not people's *feelings!'*

    AND: He don't care nothing about you *(being* **"happy"** *–* **He wants you To BE** (SAVED). "<u>God wants you/*me* to be happy</u>", is the (biggest) ploy–the enemy has come up **with** (*In the* 21st Century), modern times!

[If] you: "seek ye, first the LORD/YAHWEH, and HIS KINGDOME: [Matt: 6:33• then you can **see** what/ever type of "happiness" *H*e will "add" to you, af*ter*, [Luke 22:], "you get converted." – v.32.)

-

So, let's remember; just because YHWH is quiet with "gifts" in operation: without "their" (repentance), doesn't mean there won't be consequences.

-

Lord; help us LORD**!**
*Because ***He*** repenteth not, (of Giving them to you and me): [for now]: but the day of reckoning; i.e. "the day of the LORD", is coming, and – the great White Throne seat of judgment / day, of separation [Matt KJV 13:30], is Coming. -*
[*then there will be weeping and gnashing of teeth* – (Matt 8:12).

-

Let's make sure, holiness, and **clean** hands; & *o*bedience – *A*ccompany **our** "gifts." (So, let's get Back to your ***Authority*** - Now – that we have covered, The *GIFT*S (warning • Label.)

Rebuking kings:
*   *Asa; Saul; Ahab; Herod **(by John,** Baptist);* an endless list.

Who was it, that walked into the king's palace; *walked right up / into the king's chambers and told Hezekiah *(king)* he was going to die..? – You're right! A Prophet.
We say-what-He Say*s*.

- *DANIEL 9:6*(KJV).
[6] Neither have we hearkened unto thy servants the **prophets**, which spake in thy name to our **kings**, our princes, and our fathers, and to all the people of the land.

Psalm 105:14 – 15;

14 "He suffered(*allowed*) no man to do them wrong: yea, he reproved **kings** for their sakes;

15 Saying, Touch not mine anointed, and do my prophets no harm."

Did y'all see the correlation? YAH rebuked and brought down kings, on behalf; of: – Prophets!

(He chastised or rebuked kings, for prophets.

Who ordains 'kings', in the Bible, on the *Most High's* behalf? (***We're still** talking* ABOUT, the authority; and the ***security clearance:*** (prophets have and carry!).

- Let me put into layman's terms: a babe in Christ, sitting out in the audience/congregation cannot consecrate me as a Bishop. – (Order says, ordination flows from the head down: Which means, if MOST HIGH uses prophets for the setting/establishing of kings: then (true) prophets have a greater clearance than a king does, *Most High*), by YAHWEH:

Which is (**not**) to be interpreted, that once the Most High uses you to establish them, (or, concerning those He ***has*** established in (kingship); pastorship, (etc.), that you are not supposed obey them that *have rule over you*: -Don't mistake, nor twist it:

And just because you're a prophet, with ***greater*** clearance: (for kings), does not mean, you don't subject yourself to your local church Pastor that *YHWH* has called you to sit under, (You are not exempt), (**prophet**): don't let them fool you, (through pride).

•(You) need a pastor. - Don't fool yourself!

- *SUB-SECTION:*-(END.)

David & Nathan

He fought "kings", for the prophet's = a greater order:

1. **VERBAL WARNING**

[Please SEE: Revisit Display of Scripture of EZKL. In Cp. 2.]

*(Ever wonder why **it was a prophet** (Samuel); Sent and anointed somebody to become a 'king', (David:)*
A higher authority = than even "kings". That's our office: But we use discretion, wisdom, and OBEDIENCE:

*[2 Sam. 12:1–7; (7b – 9, 10, 11-**13**).]*
1 And the Lord sent Nathan unto David. And he came unto him, and said unto him, There were two men in one city; the one rich, and the other poor.
2 The rich man had exceeding many flocks and herds:
3 But the poor man had nothing, save one little ewe lamb, which he had bought and nourished up: and it grew up together with him, and with his children; it did eat of his own meat, and drank of his own cup, and lay in his bosom, and was unto him as a daughter.
4 And there came a traveller unto the rich man, and he spared to take of his own flock and of his own herd, to dress for the wayfaring man that was come unto him; but took the poor man's lamb, and dressed it for the man that was come to him.
5 And David's anger was greatly kindled against the man; and he said to Nathan, As the Lord liveth, the man that hath done this thing shall surely die:
6 And he shall restore the lamb fourfold, because he did this thing, and because he had no pity.
*7 And Nathan said to David, **Thou art the man**. Thus saith the Lord God of Israel, I anointed thee king over Israel, and I delivered thee out of the hand of Saul;*
8 And I gave thee thy master's house, and thy master's wives into thy bosom, and gave thee the house of Israel and of Judah; and if that had

been too little, I would moreover have given unto thee such and such things.

9 Wherefore hast thou despised the commandment of the Lord, to do evil in his sight? thou hast killed Uriah the Hittite with the sword, and hast taken his wife to be thy wife, and hast slain him with the sword of the children of Ammon.

10 Now therefore the sword shall never depart from thine house; because thou hast despised me, and hast taken the wife of Uriah the Hittite to be thy wife.

11 Thus saith the Lord, Behold, I will raise up evil against thee out of thine own house, and I will take thy wives before thine eyes, and give them unto thy neighbour, and he shall lie with thy wives in the sight of this sun.

12 For thou didst it secretly: but I will do this thing before all Israel, and before the sun.

13 And David said unto Nathan, I have sinned against the Lord. And Nathan said unto David, The Lord also hath put away thy sin; thou shalt not die.

So, David, as being only one recipient of a plethora of examples of (kings); or people in high places: - That a many, where he served as king, but a prophet, had the authority to shift him, and rebuke him, and call out his transgression: I'LL talk more about this, in **Chapter 4,** (briefly), but from a different perspective:

But that's not all the types of correcting*'s* **we do:**

2. **Prophet*(s)* RESTORES ORDER /** CORRECT **UNDERSTANDING**

(Again, *this book* is the *work* of that.)

"Laying hands" – while "trying" to (*cast out a demon), is a No – No. - For some of us, (The demon is (**not***) being stubborn, because you don't have the "power":)/ **he** *sees you don't know - What **you're** doing*! - You don't know ORDER.
(He sees that) So <u>he</u> 'rebels' you:

– *In the Book of Acts, a spirit/demon is called, 'he': (which is in the same scripture, we're about to visit.)*

• HERE's Our Cornerstone:
St Matthew *chapter* **8,** *vs.* **16, 32.**
[16]*) When the even was come, they brought unto him many that* **were possessed with devils: and he cast out the spirits with his Word,** *and healed all that were sick: -*
[in another instance: **Same chapter,** DEALING With "Another" *demon, completely: -*

[32A] *) "**And he said unto them, Go."** . .
(He never touched them:)

• Here's His team:
ACTS *cp.*16: [16]And it came to pass, as we went to prayer, a certain damsel possessed with a spirit of divination met us, which brought her masters much gain by soothsaying: [17]The same followed Paul and us, and cried, saying, These men are the servants of the most high God, which shew unto us the way of salvation. [18]And this did she many days. But Paul, being grieved, turned and **Said** to the spirit, *I command thee in*

the name of Jesus Christ to come out of her. **And** <u>he</u> **came out** the same hour.**"** -- (So; where'd y'all get *hands* from(*?*): – *sigh*.

(It wasn't THE BIBLE, and it wasn't the life of Christ.

-    *Stop that.*

-

Here: I'm tempted to talk about how people (in the *Body* of *CHRIST*), thinks That Everyone is SUPPOSED to BE MARRied: (When **Jesus**); (SAID.. It's Better Not To Be: Matthew 19:10-12:

•

But IMMA LEAVE That Alone:
(Apparently, *GOD / YHWH* is preventing me: Because maybe He wants / would Have me to do a deep *dive on that (Study),* outside of this Material: *[for you all to Receive]*: '(I'm really coming into myself in this season: and who I am: (to) the body of CHRIST:.
*((N*obody BUT-JESUS *'s-vessel))*: in ***Him***-I Live:
(USE ME **LORD**.)

-

3. *Correction of **THINGS** that **Look Like** Miracles*
• "ELISHA and the axe head."
[*This entire book was initiated from this **Preface.** (My Origin story) , **and** (+) then, YAHWEH Telling Me to tell* it*: to write THIS* BOOK!]

In 2 King. (Elisha, being the new head of the **"school of prophets",** *which biblically; the eldest track record, is that Samuel started this 'school of the prophets';* - We don't see any other schools in the Bible, other (than with) Elijah: we don't know if this was a continuation of Samuel's building *up* or if "Elijah" had started his own *at (some) / this point*: but after (Elijah) was "taken up", (Elisha) ran the show; <u>and the school</u>: (This is where we find ourselves in the text:). **- [2 Kings 6]**

• [*We'll be reading from the* Amplified Bible, 'Classic' Edition. (*AMPC*)

(King James says the same thing: I didn't have to pull from another edition: [just to prove an 'altered' point: - Because some editions are untrustworthy). • The Holy Bible said the sons of the prophets lived, with Elisha. – "(AMP)", says "*live near you*":
[*The whole reason they were trying to build* a 'new place' *in the 'first place', was because the house they lived (in)* "with" Elisha, was too small for the capacity of all his 'sons'; (meaning his students.)] – please learn how to read the *KING JAMES,* so you won't be led away from truth.

- Please be filled with the *HOLY GHOST* so you can interpret what you're reading (***even more importantly.***)

II Kings 6:*1 – 7 (AMPC)*

1 THE SONS of the prophets said to Elisha, Look now,
the place where we live before you is too small for us.
2 Let us go to the Jordan, and each man get there a
[house] beam; and let us make us a place there where we
may dwell. And he answered, Go.
3 One said, Be pleased to go with your servants. He
answered, I will go.
4 So he went with them. And when they came to the
Jordan, they cut down trees.
5 But as one was felling his beam, the axhead fell into the
water; and he cried, Alas, my master, for it was borrowed!
6 The man of God said, Where did it fall? When shown
the place, Elisha cut off a stick and threw it in there, and
the iron floated.
7 He said, Pick it up. And he put out his hand and took it.

-

(KJV) – [6] *"And the man of God said, Where fell it? And he shewed*
him the place. And he cut down a stick, and cast it in thither; and
the iron did swim."

- o First of all, the axe was borrowed: (this *'son'* / man /
  (prophet), who was in "school" to become one: he had
  no money to pay it back – THERE was something that
  needed *'fixing'*. – (THE *Situation*).
- o *Secondly: (THIS SITUATION), was about the right*
  tools (necessary) for the job at-hand: - (they were
  chopping down trees, to build *where* there was a need:
  WHAT *they needed.* (Something needed to be
  "corrected". Because how can I cut down, without an
  axe:*(?)* without the axe; there's no "access" to the trees,
  for (use) - to make out of *them,* wood: *with no wood, I*

can't build (this house), - *and now I have no axe: (and plus),* it was *borrowed: - (it wasn't even "mine:")!*

• *But have no fear; <u>the</u> "<u>prophet</u>" is Here: (!!)*

○

When Jesus spit, and made clay, that was (Jesus), "The Prophet." • (Jh 9:6) **He was correcting something.**

○

Notice: [*With both [He] and Elisha; (they both 'took' natural elements (from the Earth); and made a "miracle!"*

• *That is the Prophet's 'element'!*

• *Elisha took a stick/(wood)* from a 'tree', *and made iron to 'swim.'*

• ***Prophet (Messiah) Jesus*** *took his spit, (added) 'natural'- **dirt** of the (earth), and made eye salve.*

- (Remember when Moses; (*(Prophet)*Moses – that is), used a "stick:" (through the power/authority of Yah: •

• (we "ain't" talkin' • (witchcraft), 'backdooring'-it, (***soothsaying*** practices), - but by the power of **YHWH**; <u>connected to the Earth</u>: these **men** did these things: ***Moses*** used a stick <u>*to*</u>: - (*Isaiah 43:16b:* - ":<u>*make a way in the sea, and a path in the mighty waters;*</u>") c.f. [Ez.14]

- Then ***the LORD*** used Moses and he took that (same) ***stick***, in the - *"wilderness"; (where the people would have been dying of THIRST,* – AND struck a rock (another natural Earthen element:(the rock). - at *the LORD's* command: and water gushed out. (**Ex. 17:6**). •

- – **He was correcting**:

- (They had a need, Moses (the)Prophet, corrected it at the LORD's [empowering], and *releasing* to *him* the intel(!)

When (**Jesus)** raised a dead boy to life, [in **Luke 7**]; it wasn't just a 'miracle', *He* was "correcting" something! [*LUKE 7:12 – 16.*]

12|Now when **he** came nigh to the gate of the city, behold, there was a dead man carried out, the (<u>only</u>) son of his mother, and she was (a widow): and much people of the city was with her.

13|And when ***the Lord*** saw her, **he** had compassion on her, and said unto her, *Weep not.*

14|And **he** came and touched the bier: and they that bare *him* stood still. And **he** said, *Young man, I say unto thee, Arise.*

15|And he that was dead sat up, and began to speak. And **he** delivered him to his mother.

16|And there came a fear on all: and they glorified God, saying, That a **great prophet** is risen up among us; and, That God hath visited his people.)

• [Luke 7:12 – 16, (KJV)

There's a lot to unpack *here: but the main point happens right here, in **verse**. 12:* [*the woman* at hand, was a widow, **i.e.** (she had a husband that had died: now, the "son", had to become the man *of the* house, *(is what this means),* and "provide": work; etc. (Then, - he died!) Her (only son).

Maybe this is the very reason "compassion", (*as a particular type),* showed up in this moment, *in v.13.* • In *(14),* He gave the commandment: • *(15),* he arose, - (but even *though* this IS THE Holy Messiah: *The only **begotten** Son of 'GOD';* (even SCRIPTURE, • in -Verse [16] tells us **what** was in (operation),

- Jesus, *the* "great prophet": – A *Prophet,* who, -was ***correcting*** *SOMETHING: (*Jesus, I Love you:*).*

- **Jesus**, raising this boy, was bringing *provisioning* back into their household: *along* -with his *breath.*
  - (Jesus), you are so *Good to me.*
    (*y'all getting it?*)
- ? [REMEMBER the book cover, that **said** I would *write this book like* a **conversation piece**:[?]

- • That's why I'm speaking so loosely; *using slang,* and *speaking* not so much 'scholarly' with my vocabulary: [I could use magniloquent words: but I don't want to: this is *a* lot of information. So, I want it, as *down* to *EARTH* and *digestible* as possible.] •The (information) *you're getting; is not* only scholarly; *through the* (school) of the **HOLY GHOST**; – but it is (*STELLAR*).

- So; there's an even trade for me to "***talk***" *or, rather (speak) this loosely –* 'in a book'!

Speaking of (this) *great* **prophet**, (our) Messiah – (***Luke 7:16***) :

(**Did you know that Jesus was a**

Pastor, prophet, Teacher, Evangelist: (*?*),

- PASTOR • John *10*:*11,14,16.*
- PROPHET • Mark **6**:*3,4,* (*c.f.,* - Mt.21:11.)
- TEACHER • John **3**:*2; 13*; John **13**:13, c.f. (Mt. 23:8)·
- EVANGELIST *(it's all through the text,* the places *H*e walked through)*

(HOLY MESSIAH)

- And **only** *He*), *is* the - "***Chief Apostle***".
- **Who established ('*The'*)** CHURCH**. –** (*Hebrews 3:1*).

[If you are not establishing church*es*; **or, a' church.** *I.e.,* (*Church founder, planter: BY YAH's Commissioning, that is)*, you're not even '**a**' *apostle*.

(Away with these unbiblical proclamations we're making (ourselves.)

-

Chief apostle!

• Funny.

4. **THE** "**Rain**:"

We control weather, and 'call down fire:'
(HAVING Access to elements: **earth**: *('dirt')*; **wind**;
*water; or **fire, is** **not** a form of (Correcting), but can
be used "<u>interchangeably</u>": for that purpose: THE
GREAT JESUS / Prophet "who *walked on water;
wasn't correcting, someone else's "**problems**": but
using the element of water, (and his feet:),* Jesus, did
"**correct**" *the fact – that he had no*
TRANSPORTATION; *(**Mt.** 14:22 – 26):*
*•See, (HE sent them away, (then the multitude: then
into the mountain, to pray, (so **he** can finally: mourn,*
JOHN (the Baptist), – v.(13); after spending all day,
trying to get to that point: (*but the people followed
Him when they saw him earlier that noon day:*) then
had compassion on them, (and preached); and more,
(feeds them; all five thousand: (+) women and
children. – Then finally after mourning (through
prayer and worship (v. 23 *c.f.*) –he's ready to be joined
with his team members, *(disciples): but there's no
boat to get across: - so he walked on* **water** to **Cor**rect
*the situation. - Jesus, the 'Great **Prophet'** •* Luke 7:16.

- *Which* brings me to the next and [final.]
    - *(This will make* sense why I did this, this way,
      shortly, rather than expounding on other elements
      and people.)
    -

(**the amount of information** *YHWH* **is having me share**
(here) **with y'all;** is *literally* **scary : I did not** (KNOW He
was going to make me do all this: and actually, I'm learning
with y'all: because *THE HOLY GHOST Is – my Teacher:*

and HE's unlocking (another) level of the **prophet** *in* **me**
That I didn't know was in there: *WHILE* teaching you all,
on the level of what *I* was ALREADY *'aware' of, or that* I
carried in me-in [*some*] way.

• ("GIVE, AND IT SHALL be **given** UNTO YOU;")
- **Luke 6:38**A.

-

Thank You, (My "Great"
MESSIAH! (Jesus.)

5. Multi-functional: **<u>INTERRELATED</u>** (<u>Correcting</u>)

[Let's see how I can *do* this: Without making this lengthy!]

We'll be visiting • [***I KINGS 17:1***]

(I think this is a great way to close this segment, and close *this* chapter. And tie in *"Reporting for Duty"-* '<u>s</u> focal point, (at least, a *segment* of it: - (*You'll see:*.)

In chapter one: *we talked about the Prophets mission is to [arrest], in <u>one</u> of his/her functions: whereas, when YHWH* sends us in with a **"ticket"/**(arrest)**;** *which* the (*Recipients*) are *then* summons to *the* **"court"**, (***from*** initial-infraction / ***for*** the final *verd*ict)**; ..** [In One example] the **Multi-f**unctional operation shows up through (judgment) and (reversal). -

So not only do we have **access** to elements, (in the name of Jesus: [*I'm not talking about 'no' •voodoo; hoodoo: strange fire*, (anything), to be clear, (Again), (We don't-*dabble*: we stay holy, because all I HAVE need, is in Jesus: (I don't need a *false* power; When *he HAS* all power: (Don't play with this information and think you can run off on the plug: (Matter *of* fact: "<u>may the LORD, - Jesus Christ, keep this information concealed from all the unprocessed people, and who have another spirit, and who-would practice</u> • <u>strange fire:</u> (with) something that is come from High, and given to *those who* are relentless, - *that* **Jesus** is the only "way"! (truth) and (life). [Don't <u>play with this</u>: because this is **'Holy'**, WHO Is (Giving you this information:) *A* priest died trying to touch something that was *holy* when he wasn't-*as* much: • Don't play with this ark, people of **Yah**: [In the name of Jesus, Christ:]" • — -

(So we can use <u>*elements*</u>, as the Lord permits: But sometimes, (they) coincide, and interact/INTERCHANGE: with **the - (judgments)**!

Jesus, *(this is good). You are teaching me beyond what I even realized, I carried: [This is phenomenal: don't you all agree).? [In the ministry, using the life of the (prophet) ELIJAH.]*

I KINGS 17:1

*And Elijah the Tishbite, who was of the inhabitants of Gilead, <u>said unto Ahab</u>, As the LORD God of Israel liveth, before whom I stand, there shall not be dew nor rain these years, but according to **my** word.*

- The same Elijah who used the **fire** *element* to produce a judgment, i.e., *a* verdict to burn up and kill the prophets of Baal: i.e., '*lying*' prophets: ('proclamators': – who were not *Yah*'s.

- The same ELIJAH (just said), YAH gave me the power over #elements, #*for* the sake of your #Judgments: to king(Ahab.)

- Jesus this is good: [I'm sorry y'all. I'm receiving this portion *in real time*: ('watch me work': ha-ha: (I'm just kidding:' The 'Holy Ghost', is working, -•- I ain't nobody, I'm just being light hearted: due to my excitement about what *YHWH* is/HAS reveal**ed** to me, for **us** to use: as He gives COMMAND - and PROCESS *us* to *this* level!

In case you're not getting it: (Elijah used the power of the ***elements, to BRING judgment: (stop the rain), and the same elemental power; to unstop the (judgment),*** *and* (CORRECT) THE SITUATION, **interchangeably:** - by sending the rain (element) again: (stopping the plague of the drought!!!)

❖ *– The Judgement:*

no rain; causing draught; then famine, (by Elijah stopping, - '***the element*** of rain': "according to (my) word." - *1 Kings 17:1*

❖ ***The reason:***

- 17 And it came to pass, when **Ahab** saw **Elijah**, that Ahab said unto him, Art thou he that troubleth Israel?

- **18** <u>And he answered</u>, I have not troubled Israel; but *thou*, and thy father's house, in that ye have <u>forsaken the commandments</u> of the LORD, and thou hast <u>followed Baalim</u>.*" - 1 Kings 18:*

❖ *The CORRECTION:*

41. And Elijah said unto Ahab, Get thee up, eat and drink; for there is a sound of abundance of rain. **42**. So Ahab went up to eat and to drink. And Elijah went up to the top of Carmel; and he cast himself down upon the earth, and put his face between his knees, **44**. And it came to pass at the seventh time, that he said, Behold, there ariseth a little cloud out of the sea, like a man's hand. And he said, Go up, say unto Ahab, Prepare thy chariot, and get thee down, that the rain stop thee not. *– 1 Kings 18:41-42, 44*

And this was *after* three years from the judgment of "no rain": (that) Correction, has come:

*" And it came to pass <u>after many days</u>, that the word of the LORD came to Elijah in <u>the</u> **third year**, saying, Go, shew thyself unto Ahab; and I will **send rain** upon the earth." – 1 Kings 18:1*

[The multi-functional DOUBLE EDGED SWORD kind:*]*

No wonder the *EARTH is 'waiting on the **Manifestation** (of the sons of GOD:' (V. 19)* She wants you to know your power, and *your*-connection you have to HER: - #***Elements:***.

❖ She *travaileth and groaneth, for you to use her (Rom. 8:22)*
- *Because just like the sheep;* **(we)** hear *HIS Voice:*
- *THE EARTH, (Is Listening, for yours. • (ELEMENTS!!)*
  - *THIS is divine revelation, only for you to use when, through CHRIST;* **he's** GIVEN *you thy '**Dominion**'. (PROPHETS, we got some (work) to do to* (come) *to this* level.*)

(This *isn't* witchcraft, IT'S SUPERNATURAL. This is BIBLE.)

•

THE RAINBOW *of* CORRECTION.

•

-

Now I have set the premise, and *your eyes too* will be able [to *see: when "correction",* is in operation.]

And (*as you can see):* I'm not *talking about* "you did something wrong", *- but (all kinds) of all types.* **Now**, *I* won't bore you with countless examples in the BIBLE: but you get it:. (Or we'll be here *all day:*

-

"And there are also many other things which Jesus did, the which, if they should be written every one, I suppose that even *the world* itself could not contain the *books that should be written.* Amen."
– (John 21:25) KJV

I got a feeling; some of us wouldn't mind **being here**.
But soak it up, church! – We need <u>the</u> (<u>prophet</u>) "working:"
*This is what makes you important: you got revelation of mysteries locked up inside of you: (**<u>Amongst</u>** <u>other</u> <u>things</u>.)*

- <u>and</u> (they) think our only purpose, is to 'Prophesy.'!

CHAPTER 4.
YOUR CALLING
HOW DO YOU KNOW
WHEN YOU'RE A PROPHET

CHAPTER Four: (*4*)
How Do You KNOW When You're A Prophet

(THIS Is A very short cp.)

If the former wasn't good enough, or *did not cut it*: - or *if* it did, but you're still found wanting, - (to be *sure this is your (category)*: *Here's a few more ways I've come to terms*: That you can **identify**. (with *the* questions), if (you're A prophet).

Let's discuss some very important ways: *in* an even more relax*er* – fit, to (determine) **that**:

–   Prophet[s] are truth-tellers:

–   And we can't stand (dysfunction).

Oh AND, (Here's a wisdom nugget: fairly new too/to me:

"*PROPHET*", <u>because we are 'professional'</u>, fault–finders:

(*I don't mean that in a negative connotation,* it's just a *play* on words, on what we*'ve* already discussed:
- I*'ve come* to the discovery of best • practice:

(Observing a particular family member; I found that he, not having (in)sight, causes him to be in denial about some of the *simplest things: – I took that and *in*-turn, used it to (my) advantage: - that out of this observation, (the **LORD**) GIFTED me, with a Gift: because I ASKED (The)LORD; and out of me, came these words: - "Lord, grant(?) me self-awareness:"*

Being a prophet is so important that (*you*) **and** (*I*)**, have** (**THAT**).
–   I Believe it Is something we should (add) to our regular prayer flow of REQUESTS; *for* our "personal" *SELVES.* - *until*; (self-awareness), "you and me(**see**)" - **it's budding,**
–   (BECAUSE: - *"the Blind cannot lead, the Blind:"* (**Matthew 15:14**)*: you need to be able to (SEE) Yourself!*
    •   ------------------------- *[*II Cor. 13:5*]*

"We're Built to Tell you the TRUTH!"

The <u>Gift</u> of The *Spirit*, (of **prophecy**), -
COMPARED - (*to*) "People Who *are*
PROPHET'*s*:

-

.

"You're going to get a house", is a tell-tell sign: the "gift" of prophecy, is in operation: (anytime an individual is being 'prophesied' to), it's a *tell-tell* sign, the office of the (factual) prophet, is not present, /*(or)* in operation:

Why do I say this, because this is what prophet's, prophesying look like:

First-all; (**remember**); they already go in; **knowing what They're going to say**: "go and Tell My <u>people</u>". (This), that, ***etc.***

Secondly, (speaking of '['people'], prophet's prophesy to nations: and national facto*rs; Remember I said this.?
(WE'RE aLMoST Done, Y'aLL.)

So; when **A Prophet** *(is)* prophesying–prophesies, he's talking to a multitude: (a church, a nation, and *if *, an individual; - it's an individual who has ruling authority, - (over other's!)
- That's *a* **prophet**:

(when *YHWH sends* a prophet to speak to an *individual: about an individual: it is very seldom: - unless they have (ruling authority)/ people under them:)*
(One last time: – *like the apostle:* Cp.2 - (p.62) (he's a Pastor)*: meaning he's leading other individuals. And "God" set me up for - or to have him lay hands on me: So "GOD" can rebuke a person "gifted", but (**denying** his 'purest' anointing),[not consecrated]: (while **caring** for other people, **at** that time:.*

(In General): This is why "prophets" can rebuke "pastors": *they are people who have authority - rule over Others: Righteousness **exalts**; sin is a reproach. (Proverbs **14:34** excerpt.)*

-

[in just a second: I'll tell you,
how (you) carry *nations*:]

We're *almost done.*

You Are Tailored:

Not *Every*one gets your blessing:

(Luke 4:25, 26 KJV.)

— Let alone (they know) that it even exists.

- If they can't honor, - they can't "*get*."

This puts a whole new meaning to "*A* prophet's reward.",

• And what that looks like: and means.

That's why it's **secluded**: because you can only get the reward, if you first: "see" it: And you can "honor" it:

— Recognize it: because most prophets are cloaked, with people that are their (local.)

I remember: (as I mentioned, in *THIS MUST BE DOCUMENTED, (Book in 2020), that;* in *2019*; how **YAH** said to me, "*How do you think* **Gideon** *got close enough to the "groves", to (tear them down) in the first - place*?") – then; – told me, I was *His secret* weapon.

• (That's you.!) •

Though we hear *of* such great miracles of the two prophet's Elijah; *Elisha: - [and other's]*, (**JESUS** *Puts it in context*: and *says*, (although, - they were not given to everybody.)

It's [like the statement: "*quality over quantity*": • When we read isolated stories; *about how the prophet's*: Did *this*, or / *that!*: (it makes us feel like it was **"quantity"**, in operation, *when in* reality; not everyone was privileged, to experience an 'Elisha'; even though, he lived • '*right* down the street':

Like Jesus, in his hometown: *"ain't that JUST (Mary)/Joseph's boy" – and; they were offended! - (**Mark 6:3/4**)*

*St. Luke **4***:

24 And he said, Verily I say unto you,
No prophet is accepted in his own country.

*25 But I tell you of a truth, **many widows were in Israel** in the days of **Elias**(**Elijah**), when the heaven was shut up three years and six months, when great famine was throughout all the land;*
*26 **But** unto **none** of them was Elias sent, **save** unto Sarepta, a city of Sidon, unto 'a' woman that was a widow.*
*27 And many lepers were in Israel in the time of Eliseus(**Elisha**) the prophet; and **none** of them was cleansed, **saving Naaman** the Syrian.*
"**Save**", (means; *"except"/'(only)"*.

"-How do you know that you're a prophet:-" because only a select few, know what you (carry), and gleam from the recognition: *(locally); while several - many others (**walk past you** like you're scum, - (THE **lowest of the Kingdome's - totem pole!**) THAT's HOW They treat you!! **And they have no clue, YOU'RE** the MOST HIGH's Secret weapon, (When **"you" - got their miracle!)***
Remember, again, verse 24, (of this same chapter), as pre-text: (and Matt. 13:57; 'except':
No prophet, except, (**('Save')**)(them local people), locally.

INTERNATIONAL ••
You mesh well with *people* of other countries:
   –   They find you attractive, (extremely.)
Or; in another context, take you under their grip/*wings* if they're older, - or want to be around you, if they're younger.

Speaking of INTERNATIONAL:

(e)very <u>prophet</u>, has the 'ability for *nations*', in them:

{[in other words: **There would no need for**, "the *office of the prophet*"; if it was only meant: to be **ignored**; disrespected, undervalu*ed*, and unappreciated: (all things a prophet *deals* with, around local people, / local / '*common*', to them),

•

[Therefore: if a prophet truly has honor, of those of other nationalities, (or far away **States**; at (*the*) least: - then, that is because that is who they are called to, [**most**]: [in *time*], in most cases: [not (*a*) one size fits all: (as a matter of fact:

YHWH told Ezekiel: if I sent you to other (nation's) people: Surely, they would hear you, but (because; - I'M SENDING *YOU* – to your own people: they're 'gonna' dishonor and disrespect you: Just as they have done **Me**: (says *the* **LORD.**)

BUT: Remember when Jesus said if they receive/*reject,* (you); they receive/or/*reject* the One who sent you, (*CHRIST*); and if (Christ), they've rejected the ONE who sent Him: (the – *the* ALMIGHTY **HAYAH:** *:*

- *(other nations)* is where 'I'/WE thrive, because "unbelief" doesn't lock up the prophet's power!

Every prophet has the *(ability)* to go to nation's: *that's what you were created for, [was created in you.]*

   – *You ARE* **a prophet unto nations.** [**if**] *you are a PROPHET. (whew – wee) [how about that]!*

And another thing; don't let this region, (U.S.), and *the* (unlearned), *or* sometimes: *(demonic)* oppression; - fool you:
   – Because a lot of people like to say: ('*you don't Have to announce, who you are'),* and try to manipulate you: to shrink!
   – (Well; if you won't *know* who you are, who will**?** And: I have one question:

- HOW many times, (**in the scripture**), (Did Paul, announce himself, as an 'apostle':[?] • He wasn't being Prideful: He was ("announcing", what 'gift' is in operation), so (you) won't misalign, or misdiagnose that: (How many "Facebook" posts have you created, and people had an opinion, because they didn't understand; "the announcement", - that A prophet was speaking: (and I don't literally mean, "saying" you're a *prophet* ([unless called for]), on your "Facebook" post, - I MEAN; (and ; Again); the church "not: knowing what a prophet is: so, **when** you speak: the church (**may**) know the function, 'operation', or 'administration',

- *(1 Corinthians 12:3,4,5,6),*

which is speaking!

Sometimes: "the prophet", is speaking (judgement), and some other Christian, shows up with an opinion, because their expectation, for you, is to be speaking as if you're speaking from their lens of what they *think* a 'man of GOD', is: - a *[(*blanketed statement*)]*: which the interpretation to them, (that "a man of GOD", is caring: protecting: all the feats you think of, about your shepherd/(the) "pastor": - and that's not one-size-fits-all *either*: the "MAN OF GOD": SHOWS operation in multiples facets:

(So: (and again); When Paul starts *his letters* **off: (with)** "Paul, an apostle of Jesus Christ": (**before he says another** (**word**); he's** setting up: which–**five**-fold ministry, is getting **ready to function: The purpose and the** calling of an *(apostle)* is getting ready:-to-'operate': an ((ope**ration**)).

-No; the prophet (corrects), *but your lack of understanding wants me to operate in another zone*, (**due to your short sightedness) that** *YAH* • didn't call me to: !

- Don't Let them box you in:
- Don't let them do that to you!

(Announce who you are: so, the church can know:

 That *the* next words that are coming out of *your* mouth is from **that** function: and from *that* operation.

(My next book for example: if *YHWH Gives me grace: may be the operation of an apostle:*

(I'm not saying that I can "appropriate", – or "code switch": I'*m* saying *this* from the perspective: that I **am** an apostle: THEREFORE, I (can) speak *as one:)*

And that my point, **is** *I may not even mention being* a *prophet: (when the prophet is not in operation) - just to give you context: That what (office) showing up,* determines the **them***e*!

All *operations,*

are not the

same.

END.

(JAN 27, 2026.)

The *office* HAS **Corrected.**

(Notes)

ECCLESIASTES 12:13.

13<u>Let us hear the conclusion of the whole matter: Fear God, and keep his commandments: for this is the whole duty of man.</u>

-

Father, I declare in the Body of ***CHRIST***, CHANGE.

.. In the name of (Jesus).

BIBLIOGRAPHY

Scripture: *See Copyright page*

The Holy Bible, Conteyning the Old Testament and the New: Newly Translated out of the Originall Tongues, and with the Former Translations Diligently Compared and Revised, by His Majesties Speciall Commandment. Appointed to be Read in Churches. London: Robert Barker, 1611. [1611 KJV Apocrypha section]

The Apocrypha, Taussig, H. (2021, September 11). Are There More than 66 Books in the Bible? Early Christian Texts. https://earlychristiantexts.com/how-many-books-in-the-bible/ (Page 13,)

D.K. Williams was born having his mother's maiden name, and spent many years carrying that name, until having it changed to reflect his paternal bloodline!

He is the son of John Lee Williams, Jr., and Shirley Ann (Weaver) Thurmond. As a fun fact, both his parent's share the same birthday.

Born in the USA, in the State of Georgia; city of Atlanta, *(where he was also raised)*. However, (understanding that his **heritage** is that of *(one of)* the twelve tribes of Israel (God's chosen people, historically)! - *[The depictions on the movies, of Moses, Abraham; Jesus, are all lies!]*

His maternal Grandparents, *Willis and Ruby Weaver* had a full hand in helping Deon become the person he has come to be. - This is mainly due to the reinforcement of integrity their lives and teachings taught, in addition to his mother's raising, (in godliness), and regular church attendance.
- However, it was around the age 9 or so, that he heard the voice of the Lord, for the first time himself.
(And received his call to preach the gospel of Jesus Christ).

At the age of 18 years, the young man encountered the LORD in a manner similar to that of before, (hearing **His** voice unmistakably), but this time: more life-branding, and with much more detail! At this time, he heard the Lord speak to him that: He had called him 'into the Office of a Prophet;' - **(Which this book entails):** But was something he was totally unaware of at the time: and was-taught immediately:

(By way of asking) what the function of being one of the LORD's [true] prophets, **is: or** are all about! (?) (*"**Now, in this book, I have divulged it to you.**"* - **Say**s, *the prophet.*)

[Going back to the *Author*'s early stage:]

Deon Williams submitted himself to the process, and at age 21/22, preached, what's called his (initial), "trial sermon"; = *A chance to see if the anointing and call of God is there, as suspected by such spiritual leader(s).*

Pastor Roger Foster

[Shortly after, the young vessel stepped away from the pulpit, choosing of his own doing and will to prevent himself from becoming a hypocrite, (due to a weakness he was experiencing with an induvial at the time). And it would be eleven years before he stepped foot in another pulpit and preached the gospel again, in (that) format.]

— *"Oh, time much well spent!"* he says, growing in God.

During this time, **Pastor Gerald Bess**, pastored the young lad: from 2004 – 2012: (ages 24 – 32.)

On March 22, 2015, the minister became ordained as an **Elder** under the leadership of his *then*, 3rd and final Pastor (of His PROCESS), (2013 – 2017):

Bishop, Dr. Wilfred Durrah, Jr.., of Charity Truth Tabernacle.

His educational background all stems from the Atlanta area, including his college matriculation at the "illustrious" – *Clark Atlanta University*, where he obtained a bachelor's degree of Religion/

minor in Philosophy, - (and immediately begin to attend the seminarian master's degree program - months later after graduation!)

During his undergraduate experience, Deon started his first (music) Company, *As In Heaven, Inc.*, in August of 2014, where the slogan is "God's Sound in the Earth".

Two years later, in February 2016, (and one-year after Being called an Elder): *SOUL FOOD INTERNATIONAL MINISTRIES, Inc.*, was *'legally'* born. | www.SFIM.org.
*The instructions were to lock the name in, but go no further, as the Lord told him also, *"You won't be ready to pastor until you're 36"*. - *being 35 at the time.*
– And surely it was so! At age 36, with one month remaining before turning 37, SOUL FOOD INTERNATIONAL MINISTRIES' inaugural service was launched, (with his Bishop's BLESSING, and send-off: - September 3, 2017.
(You all are invited to join us, in worship!)

One(1) year -&- nine(9) months later into serving in his pastoral-calling, and the ministry growing: the LORD instructed Pastor Williams: to ask his Bishop- for an INSTALLATION, (so Earth can officially recognize what HEAVEN had-said: (and the reason one wasn't given initially: because *Bishop Durrah,* stated, [:since SOUL FOOD INTERNATIONAL was a *FOUNDING* Ministry, the pastor *of* that ministry didn't need an installation: into what he was establishing, (and that 'installations', are for people taking over another ministry): But "GOD" said, – call the Earth to agree with (what I, the LORD, have said: *you need a* 'official *recognition/announcement: that you are no* longer ELDER BUT **PASTOR**... and on *June 23, 2019, earth got the "announcement",* after NEARLY two years, (of already Pastoring*): -*

Bishop Durrah installed "Pastor Williams," in an official capacity:

(*By the way*, Bishop Durrah *didn't receive* an (INSTALLATION) when he was "blessed" (by his pastor) to go out some 40+ years ago to pastor his church he established, by the LORD: - *(so he was following that example, which was set for/Before him, too.*

[But GOD fixed it!]

Beyond the invitations and engagements to minister at various churches locally, the prophet has ministered for *Spy TV* in Accra, Ghana, AFRICA, during his 2020 visit to the Motherland.

His authorship was prophesied openly by a visiting prophet to the church he attended from 2004 - 2012, that Pastor Williams would author the books *someday* the theologians would read *and* study from: *"a double theologian"* he was declared to be: (Through *Prophecy!*) Also prior to, The *LORD* himself had been telling him, as a young man, to "write" for many years, but he did not understand during those earlier years, that what he was to write would be books. (There was uncertainly on what the Lord meant during those moments, frequently *throughout the years.*)

With there being nothing that 'he' deemed as pressing or specific, he put those things 'off," in disobedience; – uncertain what sorts of writing he was being commanded to write in the first place. During that season, the word of the Lord, was simply to "write."

(He later understood that season to *"write,"* was not for books *(that would later come),* but as an opportunity for sharpening and preparation of what would *(later)* be!) [Though he missed those moments in his youth, he understands the season for what it was now.]

In 2020/2021 THIS MUST BE DOCUMENTED became his First author's-ship: each year representing: A *First* & *Second* EDITION.

Let's hope that we will continue to hear of *Deon K. Williams* in this manner and fashion, as a book writer: (Prophet-Pastor, Author, DEON K. WILLIAMS), – as a continued friend of "the truth."

(Jesus *CHRIST.*) (**John 14:6**)